Advance Praise for

Voluntary Sustainability Standards: Illusions of Progress and a Way Forward

'The dominant narrative about voluntary sustainability standards is that they have benefited the first movers in the industry by improving their image, but that they have also raised the bar for whole sectors, and successfully compensated for the downward pressure on production methods resulting from global competition. This volume challenges this premature conclusion. It provides robust empirical analysis to illustrate the failures of many such standards. Its great merit is to bring to the fore the issue that most economic analyses neglect entirely: that of power in agrifood chains'.

– Olivier De Schutter, Former UN Special Rapporteur on the Right to Food (2008– 2014); UN Special Rapporteur on Extreme Poverty and Human Rights

'The rising dominance of big corporations in Asian food retail and the digitalization of their sales practices increasingly proves that it is detrimental to arresting poverty and hunger. Voluntary sustainability standards are part and parcel of these structural changes. They exclude our peasantry from evolving markets, destroy informal activities, such as in food processing and marketing, and impose on us a concept of sustainability that narrowly serves corporate interests. This book unmasks the hypocrisy of the whole exercise, providing much needed insight and analysis'.

– Lim Li Ching, Senior Researcher, Third World Network

'Voluntary sustainability standards have successfully raised awareness about the huge environmental and social problems embedded in the world's food systems. This report analyses the inherent limitations of the concept and showcases the ability of big food to use such standards for their PR-campaigns and to exclude small holders from accessing markets. The authors make a convincing case that real sustainability requires inclusive and transparent governance involving all stakeholders. Let us learn the lessons!'

– Alexander Müller, Managing Director of TMG—Thinktank; Former State Secretary (German Ministry for Agriculture) and Assistant Director-General of FAO

'It is high time that this book reviews the experience with the use and the real impact of sustainability standards. The merit of this analysis is its focus on the political economy of such standards in international supply chains and their role in transforming the international agro-food production and markets'.
     – *Prof. Ernst von Weizsaecker, Honorary President, The Club of Rome*

'The African food sovereignty movement has been tackling with the restricting impact of markets on the biodiversity of African agriculture for a long time. Reading the book, I was alerted to the importance and ambivalent role of global sustainability standards in global food markets. I learnt how, as a constituent part of the current unjust global agro-food system, Voluntary Sustainability Standards can jeopardize the food sovereignty of our African peasant-based systems and exclude our smallholders from linking to markets'.
     – *Mariam Mayet, Executive Director of the African Centre for Biodiversity, Johannesburg*

Voluntary Sustainability Standards

PETER LANG
New York • Bern • Berlin
Brussels • Vienna • Oxford • Warsaw

Ulrich Hoffmann and Arpit Bhutani

Voluntary Sustainability Standards

Illusions of Progress and
a Way Forward

PETER LANG
New York • Bern • Berlin
Brussels • Vienna • Oxford • Warsaw

Library of Congress Cataloging-in-Publication Data

Names: Hoffmann, Ulrich, author. | Bhutani, Arpit, author.
Title: Voluntary sustainability standards: illusions of progress and a way
forward / Ulrich Hoffmann, Arpit Bhutani.
Description: New York: Peter Lang, 2021 |
Includes bibliographical references and index.
Identifiers: LCCN 2021013731 (print) | LCCN 2021013732 (ebook)
ISBN 978-1-4331-8771-1 (hardback) | ISBN 978-1-4331-8772-8 (ebook pdf)
ISBN 978-1-4331-8773-5 (epub)
Subjects: LCSH: Food industry and trade—Standards. | Food industry and
trade—Environmental aspects. | Nutrition policy. | Agricultural
industries—Standards. | Agricultural industries—Environmental aspects. |
Agriculture and state. | Sustainable agriculture. | Sustainable
development. | Sustainable development reporting. | Environmental policy.
Classification: LCC HD9000.5 .H597 2021 (print) | LCC HD9000.5 (ebook) |
DDC 338.1/90218—dc23
LC record available at https://lccn.loc.gov/2021013731
LC ebook record available at https://lccn.loc.gov/2021013732
DOI 10.3726/b18306

Bibliographic information published by **Die Deutsche Nationalbibliothek**.
Die Deutsche Nationalbibliothek lists this publication in the "Deutsche
Nationalbibliografie"; detailed bibliographic data are available
on the Internet at http://dnb.d-nb.de/.

Contents

List of Figures, Tables and Boxes		ix
Preface		xi
Acknowledgements		xv
Introduction		1
I.	Sustainability Standards, Their Systems, Role and Impact	5
	A. The Taxonomy of Sustainability Standards	5
	B. The Ambivalent Antecedents of Voluntary Sustainability	
	Standards (VSS)	19
	C. Opportunities and Benefits that Could Arise from VSS	26
	D. The Impact of VSS and the Insufficient Leverage for	
	Transformational Change	29
	E. The Limitations and Cons of VSS	38
	1. Transparency, Openness and Conflict of Interests	38
	2. VSS as International Standards and the Problem of	
	Sufficient Local Flexibility	39
	3. Inclusion or Exclusion: Can VSS Really Work for	
	Smallholder Farmers?	42

F. Can VSS-Governed Sustainability Markets Really be
    Mainstreamed and Graduate from Current Market Niches? 49
G. 'Organic' – A Standard with a Different Touch 52
    1. Evolution of 'Organic' 52
    2. What Makes 'Organic' Special? 53
    3. Basic Differences between 'Organic' and 'Other VSS' 54
    4. The Commercial Success Leads to Capitalistic
       Competition 57
    5. Inherent Contradictions 59
    6. Certification 60
    7. Conclusion 62

II. VSS at a Crossroads 63
A. What Are the Key Market Challenges, What Can VSS
    Realistically Deliver and Where Must They Fail? 65
    1. The Asymmetrical Market Power along the Supply Chain 70
    2. The Race to the Bottom 72
    3. Limited Control over a Range of Essential Flanking and
       Supportive Elements for VSS 73
    4. The Myth of Yield Increases 73
    5. Economic and Social Sustainability Remain Illusionary
       without Reforming the International Commodity Price-
       Fixing System 75
    6. Summing up 77

III. Is There Any Future Perspective for VSS and What Might It
     Look Like? 79
A. Rebalancing Power in Global Agri-food Supply Chains 80
    1. Restoration of National Supply Management: State or
       Producer Organization Driven 80
    2. Strengthening and Changing the Focus of Competition
       Policy 84
    3. Reducing the Abuse of Power: Limiting the Use of
       Restrictive Business and Trading Practices 85
    4. Legislation on due Diligence for Avoiding Precarious
       Employment Conditions, Infringement of Human
       Rights, and Environmental Damage 86

B. International Coordination and Supply Management   90
   1. The Concept of International Commodity-Related
      Environment Agreements   91
C. Lifting the Bar of Sustainability Performance: How Can
   VSS Play a Constructive Role in the Future?   94
   1. Is the Constructive Use of VSS in the European Union's
      Generalised Scheme of Preference (GSP) an Option?   95
   2. The Complementary Role of VSS to Regulation on Key
      Sustainability Issues   99
D. Epidemics and VSS: A Relationship that Is None   109
E. To Sum up   117

List of Acronyms   123
Explanations of Some Technical Terms   127
References   133
Index   143

Figures, Tables and Boxes

Figure 1: Interplay between regulation and standards   8
Figure 2: Evolution of estimated minimum production area for selected
           exported VSS-certified food commodities for the period
           2008–2018   17
Figure 3: VSS impact assessment results for cocoa and coffee producers in
           12 developing countries (comparing certified with conventional
           farmers, and reflecting the variation), 2009–2013   31
Figure 4: Market concentration in global food supply chains   70
Figure 5: Changes in the share of end consumer prices between the
           principal supply chain actors in the period 1995–2011 in percent 71
Figure 6: Long-term trend of international cocoa prices in real terms for
           the period 1952 to 2020 (in thousands 2018 US$ per tonne)   76

Table 1:   Production area of some VSS-certified commodities in 2018
           and related growth rates   16
Table 2:   Estimated minimum production volume of several VSS-
           certified agricultural commodities in 2018   17

Box 1:   The definition of standards by the WTO and ISO   6
Box 2:   Largely inconclusive discussions in the WTO on private
          standards and their trade-restrictive effects   10
Box 3:   Green consumerism: Can we really shop our way to a better
          world?   21
Box 4:   Impact assessment of VSS: Incremental versus transformational
          change   32
Box 5:   Understanding the 'Cost Treadmill Trap' and its implications
          for VSS-compliant producers   49
Box 6:   Much more sustainable cocoa production is possible – The
          example of FAIRAFRIC   68
Box 7:   The key features of the EU's GSP scheme and the applicable
          tariff preferences   96
Box 8:   The EU's Forest Law Enforcement Governance and Trade
          Program (FLEGT)   107

Preface

As neoliberal paradigms reached their climax in the 1990s and early 2000s, new narratives emerged in trade debates arguing that international supply chains would play a pivotal role in promoting global trade and economic growth. These narratives suggested that opening up the economies was not only desirable but the only way to have a meaningful participation in the world economy. Moreover, they also predicted that the intensified interdependency in international production relationships inevitably implied greater mutual policy dependency, a de-territorialization of production that called for a diminishing role of national macro-economic policy and the need of a common policy framework. Under this paradigm, less policy space will be left for countries to establish policy frameworks adapted to their needs and conditions. Instead, businesses themselves would set the rules, such as through voluntary sustainability standards that would eventually make supply chains more environmentally, socially and economically sustainable.

As discussed in this book, the reliance on businesses self-designed sustainability standards has been far from delivering the promised results. In many cases, such standards brought about market distortions or were overambitious or naïve and, ultimately, ineffective. Thus, in many agro-food sectors, the increasing use of sustainability standards de facto became a 'license to operate' that excluded certain producers from the market. In addition, despite the soaring market share of standard-compliant products, the key sustainability problems in related production and markets have neither been overcome nor significantly reduced. This ranges from deforestation and biodiversity loss, over child labour or modern slavery in social terms, to insufficient living income and wages.

There is every evidence that voluntary sustainability standards are at a crossroads. If business as usual continuous and there is a growing perception that these standards mostly boil down to greenwashing, consumers may get disillusioned on the claim that by buying certified products they can shop their way to a better world.

It is also of central importance to consider the extent to which producers, particularly in developing countries, actually benefit from those standards. Are certified products not only more environmentally suitable, but also socially and economically remunerative for producers? The analysis in this book casts considerable doubt on this. Even for sustainability standards, such as organic agriculture and fair trade, additional income gains have been modest or outright disappointing; a decent living income for farmers and farm workers continues to remain out of reach.

Moreover, while some voluntary standard programs strengthen capacity building on management and agronomic skills, the compliance with most sustainability standards requires significant investment for adjusting production and conducting conformity assessment. There is stiff competition among producers to be standard-compliant in the most cost-effective way, implying that small-scale producers get marginalized. There is, in fact, an increasing perception among producers and exporters in developing countries that sustainability standards are imposed on them with a logic and justification based on Northern preferences and conditions, fuelling the impression that a good number of these standards border on technical barriers to trade.

The claims made that voluntary sustainability standards might not only achieve the targeted sustainability goals but also self-cure some of the key systemic market flaws have turned out to be wishful thinking. The internalization of economic, social and environmental costs has not happened and in most agrofood sectors producers are faced with an even higher power asymmetry in global supply chains.

After more than three decades of increasing use of sustainability standards, a fact-based stocktaking and sober-minded analysis of their real sustainability impact was long overdue. The question is not only what was their impact but whether private sustainability standards can be made fit for a very challenging future with far-going transformations in production and consumption patterns and, particularly whether they can be more, truly sustainable. And this is unlikely to occur, as the authors conclude, without far better development and income prospects for farmers.

This book addresses these and other issues based on a thorough analysis and well-defined conceptual framework. Importantly, it not only examines the past but constructively explores whether there is a future for voluntary sustainability standards. After almost 30 years in which they have brought about more illusion than reality, it is time to rethink the role of such standards and how sustainability objectives can actually be reached.

Dr Carlos María Correa
Executive Director, South Center, Geneva

Acknowledgements

The authors would like to give special credit to and are very grateful for the extraordinary support and guidance provided by Rudolf Buntzel in brainstorming on and preparing the manuscript.

The authors would also like to acknowledge and extend special thanks to the following persons, who provided comments on earlier versions of this manuscript: Stephan Albrecht, Diane Bowen, Gareth Dale, Thomas Dietz, Nikolai Fuchs, Piter Glasbergen, Aarti Krishnan, Peter Lunenborg, Gunnar Rundgren, Bill Vorley, and Reinhard Weissinger.

Grateful acknowledgement is also made to the following institutions and individuals for granting authorization to reproducing copyrighted material: ITC, FiBL, IISD (2020). The state of sustainability markets 2020: statistics and emerging trends. Geneva; Committee on Sustainability Assessment (COSA, 2013). The COSA Measuring Sustainability Report: Coffee and Cocoa in 12 Countries. Philadelphia; Oxfam (2018). Ripe for Change: Ending human suffering in supermarket supply chains. Cowley, Oxford, UK; Fountain, A.C. (VOICE Network) and Huetz-Adams, F. (Südwind Institut). Cocoa Barometer 2020; and Marx, A., Lein, B., Sharma, A., Suse, A.G., Willemyns, I., Ebert, F. and Wouters, J. (2018). What role can Voluntary Sustainability Standards play in the European Union's GSP scheme? Leuven Centre for Global Governance Studies, University of Leuven, Leuven, Belgium.

Introduction

Whoever visits a supermarket or greengrocery these days to buy a pack of roasted coffee beans, a chocolate bar or a yogurt cup will recognize that one or several logos of sustainability standards are figuring on their outside packaging, such as Organic, Fairtrade, Rainforest Alliance or UTZ. In more and more cases, QR codes are attached to the logos so that customers can instantly get more information on the production and processing methods of the product in question and on the contents of the applied sustainability standard. As often between half and a dozen of different sustainability standards can be used for a single certified product, it is anything but easy as a lay-consumer to figure out the subtle differences between these sustainability standards.

Even so, these standards give the impression to consumers that they can 'vote with their wallets'. Sustainability standards have thus become an integral and constituent part of 'green and ethical consumerism'. Neoliberal concepts link liberty with market deregulation and individual consumption, creating the impression that identity and subjectivity are defined in terms of what is consumed and that free markets empower the consumer, and that, as a consequence, corporate conduct is driven by consumer choice.

But can consumers really shop their way to a better world?

While we should indeed buy more sustainably produced goods and services and pay a decent price for them (that internalizes at least some of the true social and environmental costs and grants an adequate livelihood to producers), there is a heated debate among academics and practitioners whether purchasing sustainability-standards-compliant products has a significant or rather small effect on social, ecological and economic change or can even usher into transformational change.

While those advocating an increasing use of sustainability standards refer to the importance of green and ethical consumerism in the context of the concepts of 'green growth' and 'green economy' or stress that despite their limits these standards are at least a good 'first step' in the right direction, others are far from persuaded by the merit of the case.

One group of critics underline that conscious consumerism is indeed a first step, but it is hard and unlikely to move on from that to anything substantive. In their view, green and ethical consumerism is not a bridge to effective social, economic and ecological change, but rather a barrier to it. It is, so the argument goes, a distraction away from recognizing the social dimensions of the sustainability problems societies face. The solution to the socio-environmental crisis is defined as individual consumer action, deflecting attention from power elites and systemic issues of the economy.

Another group of sceptics emphasize that sustainability standards as a narrative are oversold. Their main aim is to make consumers in rich economies feel good. Yet, on scrutiny, not a small number of these standards boil down to or contain elements of 'greenwashing' or de facto represent forms of 'modern indulgence trade'.

Yet other critical voices refer to the fact that the inflationary development of sustainability standards and labels is driven by vested interest and a failed attempt to minimize risk by focusing on refining standard systems rather than improving actual sustainability performance and paying due attention to the governance capacity of standards as tools for oriented social change.

Consumer surveys also suggest that label fatigue is becoming widespread and even some large companies that used to be either initiators or staunch supporters of sustainability standards two to three decades ago are reconsidering their strategies in the light of label overload and erosion of their stand-out character in the market.

At the upstream level of the supply chain, there has also been a commodification of sustainability standards. Farmers and other producers are no longer benefitting from remunerative price or quality premiums. Generally these standards have not lastingly improved the economic and social sustainability of most producers, which makes the achievement of ecological sustainability illusory.

All this said, it is high time that one reviews the role and track record of sustainability standards in contributing to true socio-economic and environmental sustainability and related transformational change, if any, since the early 1990s, when many of these standards emerged. Furthermore, one needs to explore what voluntary (private) sustainability standards as a business-level market instrument can and can't realistically achieve. In this regard it is important to focus the analysis on the contribution of sustainability standards to noticeable change in the agro-food economy and the improvement of economic sustainability and related livelihoods of producers and not the better functioning and incremental refinement of the mechanics of the standard system and the dissemination of best practice in standard compliance and use.

This manuscript attempts to conduct such review. What follows is however not a technical analysis of sustainability standards and their impact, but a review of the political economy of sustainability standard systems and their contribution to transformational change in the agro-food economy. Such standards on non-product-related processes and production methods are not simple technical tools that facilitate the exchange and trade of goods; they should rather be regarded as social governance institutions that may be used in the interest of some groups against others (e.g. for market differentiation, power asymmetries along supply chains or the shifting of costs).

The analysis in the manuscript is not confined to, but gives special attention to sustainability standards for traditional agro-food commodities, such as tropical beverages, fruit and vegetables, cereals, wood and dairy products and their role and contribution to overcoming the deep-rooted socio-economic and ecological problems in the concerned global commodity markets. These products have and are still playing an important role for the social, economic and ecological development in the Global South as well as in international trade.

It should not go without comment that the analysis in this manuscript also draws on countless personal experience one of the authors has made while working as a scholar and UN official on various clusters of sustainability standards since the 1990s. This work involved the launching of the FAO/IFOAM/ UNCTAD International Task Force on Harmonization and Equivalence in Organic Agriculture; the development of regional standards on organic agriculture in East Africa and South-East Asia; the involvement in the deliberations of the Working Group of the WTO SPS Committee on Private Standards; and the creation of the UN Forum on Sustainability Standards (a joint initiative of five

UN agencies: FAO, ITC, UNCTAD, UN Environment and UNIDO). Each of these activities lasted over several years and thus formed a body of rich experience on analysis, discussions with many governments and public donor agencies, standard creating bodies, NGOs and private sector associations related to the need for, effectiveness and impact of, benefits and challenges of, as well as limits for sustainability standards.

The manuscript is structured in three parts: part one elaborates on the standard system, recapitulates the main reasons and driving forces for the emergence of sustainability standards and reviews the pros and cons of these standards. Part two puts the spotlight on voluntary sustainability standards at a crossroads, exploring the question of what these standards can realistically achieve and where they are bound to fail. The final part three elaborates on the issue of whether there is any future constructive perspective for voluntary sustainability standards and what it might look like.

The introductory remarks would be incomplete without mentioning that due to the broad array of voluntary sustainability standards, and lack of clear criteria to qualify them, the analysis in this manuscript as a category, called voluntary sustainability standards (VSS) is challenging. Here and also in general on occasion the analysis seems to lead to overgeneralizations (i.e. the impression that all VSS are this-or-that-way when they are not) or focus on a topic applicable to only a few schemes (e.g. meaningful price premiums that are mostly in Fair Trade and Organic Standard schemes and not so much in business-to-business standards) without differentiation among schemes. This is a functional weakness of the current system, not the weakness of the analysis in this book.

I.

Sustainability Standards, Their Systems, Role and Impact

A. The Taxonomy of Sustainability Standards

Standards are typically voluntary instruments that address products, processes, systems, services, terminology, symbols, marking or labelling requirements. The purpose of standards is to provide – for common and repeated use – rules, guidelines or characteristics for activities or their results. Standards should be based on the consolidated results of science, technology, and experience,[1] and aimed at the promotion of optimum community benefits.[2]

This working definition draws on the framing and conceptualization of standards in the World Trade Organization (WTO) and the International Organization for Standardization (ISO), as summarized in Box 1.

---

1 It should not go without comment that there is some contradiction or at least tension between the demand that standards should be science-based and at the same time be developed by stakeholders and decided in a consensus-seeking process. In the experience of quite a number of interviewed experts science plays a limited role in most sustainability standards in the same way as it mostly plays a limited role in regulations.
2 This definition was proposed by Reinhard Weissinger, External Professor, University of Geneva, School of Social Sciences, and former Senior Expert, Research and Education, International Organization for Standardization (ISO).

Box 1: The definition of standards by the WTO and ISO[3]

The WTO, in its Agreement on Technical Barriers to Trade (TBT), defines a 'standard' as a

'document approved by a recognized body that provides, for common and repeated use, rules, guidelines or characteristics for products or related processes and production methods, with which compliance is not mandatory. It may also include or deal exclusively with terminology, symbols, packaging, marking or labelling requirements as they apply to a product, process or production method' (WTO, 1994).

ISO (and its partner organization, the International Electrotechnical Commission, IEC) refers to a 'standard' as

'document, established by consensus and approved by a recognized body, that provides, for common and repeated use, rules, guidelines or characteristics for activities or their results, aimed at the achievement of the optimum degree of order in a given context. NOTE Standards should be based on the consolidated results of science, technology and experience, and aimed at the promotion of optimum community benefits' (ISO and IEC, 2004).

Both definitions agree that standards are documents that are approved by a recognized body and provide rules, guidelines or characteristics, which, in the ISO-definition relate to 'activities or their results', whereas, in the WTO-definition and because of the specific focus of the TBT Agreement, are limited to products, related processes and production methods. The scope of the ISO definition is therefore wider and includes services and any other topic, such as ethical aspects of business, which are not covered by the WTO-definition. The WTO General Agreement on Trade in Services (GATS) mentions technical standards in Article VI on Domestic Regulation.[4]

There are also a number of other important differences between these two definitions: While the ISO-definition emphasizes consensus as to the basis for standards,

---

3 This box is derived from Weissinger (2021).

4 For a discussion on the role of standards and their application to services see WTO document S/WPDR/W/49 of the Working Party on Domestic Regulation under GATS, issued on 13 September 2012.

the WTO definition does not require that. Furthermore, the ISO-definition leaves the legal status of a standard open: A standard can have a voluntary or a mandatory status, whereas the WTO-definition defines that a standard is voluntary (as opposed to a technical regulation, which is mandatory).

Standards have the following functions:

- Providing rules, guidelines or characteristics for activities or their results;
- Defining terminology;
- Providing taxonomies and classification systems;
- Setting basic requirements for products and services ('fitness for use');
- Assuring compatibility and interchangeability (contributing to network effects);
- Reducing the varieties of products;
- Assuring health, safety and environmental protection; and
- Supporting organizations in their management practices.

Standards can have a different legal status, some are referred to as a 'codex' or 'technical specification', they may be part of agreements or contracts, and can be used as the basis for certificates or labels. While most standards are voluntary, some can also find their way into laws and other forms of government regulation.[5] In addition, standards can be trend setters or precursors for government regulation (see Figure 1).

Standards are widely used in regulation and legislative instruments (in particular in the EU with an elaborate system that currently comprises around 4,000 standards developed in support of regulations and legislative instruments).[6] The

---

5 Many standards adopted by the Codex Alimentarius Commission (a joint standard-setting body of FAO and WHO on food safety), the World Organization for Animal Health and the International Plant Protection Convention (the three international standard-setting organizations recognized by the WTO SPS Agreement) are taken over or translated into government regulation. Also, a good number of standards on organic agriculture were converted into regulation to safeguard the integrity of the standard claims and the organic market.

6 It should be emphasized that 'regulation' is a specific form of legislation in the EU, which is mandatory across EU-member countries without having to undergo a process of national ratification. This is different from EU directives that require national ratification and national adaptation. However, both EU regulations and EU directives can include references to standards. Although European standards are widely used in EU legislative documents, the referenced standards typically retain their voluntary status and do not become mandatory. Demonstration of compliance with the standards is only one way of showing compliance with the legal requirements in the EU.

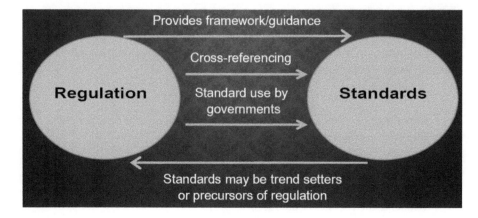

Figure 1: Interplay between regulation and standards

reference to standards in other parts of the world in areas such as safety, health, environmental protection is also widespread.

Neghi (2020) calls into question the argument of some analysts (for instance, Marx, 2017) that there is no longer any real distinction between public and private standards based on two arguments: (i) private standards are often based on public norms and (ii) when governments back private standards, they become a part of 'public' governance. Such 'incorporation by reference' is problematic because when a private standard finds government backing, ' . . . the rule becomes mandatory but the process of developing the standard remains private' (Mavroidis and Robert, 2016: 14).

Sustainability standards are standards that address a single, multiple or sometimes even systemic sustainability issues (the latter for instance under standards on organic agriculture). They fall into three clusters:

1. Sustainability standards developed by governments themselves.[7]
2. Sustainability standards developed by the formal national, regional or international standardization system, which includes ISO and its members as well as CEN (the European Committee for Standardization) and other regional standard bodies in other parts of the world. These standards can remain voluntary or can be made mandatory.

---

7 Standards on organic agriculture are mandatory in a good number of countries. In others, they are voluntary. In many countries, mandatory and voluntary organic standards exist in parallel, for instance in the EU (for more detail, see Section I.G.).

3. Sustainability standards typically developed by civil society, NGOs, combinations of companies and NGOs with occasional participation by other stakeholders outside the national, regional or international standardization system represented by ISO and its members. These standards are usually voluntary in nature, but, in few cases, may also be referenced in government legislation for meeting specific mandatory sustainability requirements. One can further sub-divide this cluster into:
   a. private 'pre-competitive' standards on best managerial or professional practice; and
   b. private company-specific standards for competitive positioning and reputation-gathering or voluntary standards set by NGOs for achievement of specific sustainability objectives .

The focus of this book are the sustainability standards of cluster 3, which are often collectively referred to as Voluntary Sustainability Standards (VSS).

Legally speaking, standards developed within the framework of the national, regional or international standardization system are voluntary, unless explicitly made mandatory by governments. However, one should demarcate these standards from those developed outside the formal standardization system, because standard development in the former follows formal rules on transparency, openness, scientific justification etc. This is why one should distinguish between the formal and non-formal system of standard creation. It should however be mentioned that some private standard-setting organizations have rules related to transparency, openness, procedure, handling of comments, complaints procedures etc. One of the key objectives of the ISEAL Alliance, for instance, is exactly the development of such principal procedures.

In short, VSS – also known as private standards, eco-labels or sustainability certificates – are standards created by the private sector, civil society organizations and (to a far lesser extent) also by governments (on ownership see below) that deal partly or exclusively with desirable or undesirable environmental, social and animal-welfare practices. The majority of VSS thus deals with (i) product or product characteristics that can be appreciated by consumers in end products or (ii) processes and production methods (the so-called credence values, which the consumer cannot appreciate in the end product) (for more detail, see Ponte and Gibbon, 2005).

Box 2: Largely inconclusive discussions in the WTO on private standards and their trade-restrictive effects

Article 4 of Annex 3 of the TBT Agreement of the WTO lays out the Code of Good Practice for the preparation, adoption and application of standards, which may be adopted by any standardizing body for the development of standards. The governments have to take reasonable measures to ensure that local governmental or non-governmental standardizing bodies do the same. If a standardizing body accepts and complies with the Code, it is considered to be complying with the principles of the TBT Agreement.

It is clear from the TBT Agreement that standardizing bodies may be governmental or non-governmental bodies, but there is no settled test for determining which bodies should be recognized as standardizing bodies or which standards may be recognized as relevant international standards.

The TBT definition of a standard refers to rules being laid down for a product (i.e. its characteristics) or related processes and production methods of a product. This has given rise to the concept of processes and production methods (PPM) and non-product related processes and production methods (NPR-PPM) standards. The distinction between them depends upon whether a method significantly alters the product characteristics. Non-product related standards typically relate to the conditions in which a product was made, the impact of the production process on the environment or the conditions of workers involved in producing the product or its constituents in this case the emissions released in the life cycle of a product, because the product is physically indistinguishable from a product made under different conditions.

Therefore, the interpretation of the TBT Agreement about the definition of a standard is not fully settled. Moreover, many VSS are likely to be NPR-PPM standards, and there is a debate about whether NPR-PPM standards are included in the TBT Agreement's definition of standards or not.

This confusion has led some developing countries to express concern that a set standard, which is thought to be voluntary can still become de facto compulsory by market power and violate the principles of non-discriminatory treatment by the WTO (i.e. the concept of like products). While the importing country thus may consider the private standard as voluntary, the exporting country often cites a nexus between private standards and public policy objectives making the situation more complex and potentially ambiguous.

In 2005, for the first time St. Vincent and the Grenadines complained to the SPS Committee about stringent requirements of private standards to banana exports to European supermarkets (see WTO document G/SPS/R/37/Rev.1, paras 16–20). In this complaint, St.Vincent and Grenadines were supported by Jamaica, Peru, Ecuador and Argentina. The EU delegation responded to that complaint by stressing that the issue was related to a private standard created and managed by a private organization. The matter should therefore be raised privately with the concerned non-governmental organization (see WTO document www.wto.org/english/news_e/news05_e/sps_june05_e.htm).

Since then many developing countries have raised concerns on these standards in various WTO bodies and their arguments have relied on Article 13 of the SPS Agreement which states that ' . . . Members shall take such reasonable measures as may be available to them to ensure that non-governmental entities within their territories, as well as regional bodies in which relevant entities within their territories are members, comply with the relevant provisions of this Agreement'. The concerns raised by developing countries can be broadly categorized as follows (see WTO document G/SPS/GEN/746, 24 January 2007):

Concerns on the content of private standards	Concerns related to compliance with private standards
Proliferation of private standard schemes both within and between markets	Cost of third party certification, particularly for small and medium-sized enterprises and farmers in developing countries
'Blurring' of official SPS-Agreement tolerated measures with private standards	Requirements of some private schemes to use only specific certification bodies
Relationship of private standards with the international standard-setting bodies referenced under the SPS Agreement	Lack of equivalence between private standard schemes leading to multiple inspection and certification requirements
Scientific justification for certain PPM requirements	Lack of recognition of certificates issued and/or lack of recognized certification bodies in developing countries

An ad hoc working group of the WTO SPS Committee discussed relevant issues of private standards in food safety and animal-plant health between October 2008 and October 2010. Discussions however largely remained inconclusive. The ad hoc working group and later the SPS Committee were even unable to agree on the definition of private standards (for the five finally agreed actions by the SPS Committee see www.wto.org/english/news_e/ news11_e/sps_30mar11_e.htm).

If one reviews the dynamics of the different kinds of sustainability standards, one finds that private voluntary and non-profit voluntary standards have been the most dynamic types since the early 1990s (Gruère, 2013: 29).

To be effectively applied, standards require a specific quality infrastructure, which is normally organized at a national level, based on internationally accepted principles that assure mutual recognition of requirements and conformity assessment results to facilitate trade and avoid multiple testing at national borders. In addition to standards, the quality infrastructure consists of the following elements:

- Metrology;
- Accreditation;
- Conformity assessment (including testing, inspection and certification); and
- Market surveillance.

Essentially, the system provides the administrative, managerial and technical infrastructure to adequately measure products (metrology), verify and identify whether and that the standard requirements are met (through testing, inspection and certification) and by ensuring that the entities that undertake the verification have themselves the required competence to engage in this function (accreditation). Through market surveillance further after-sales verification of products and services offered on the market is undertaken (see Weissinger, 2021). Quality infrastructure performs an important public policy function with regard to assuring product safety, health and environmental aspects of products, their inspection as well as for production methods.

Using agro-food products as a basis, sustainability standards can be classified applying the following constituent elements:

Guiding Element	Properties
Objective	(a) multi-dimensional: includes various facets of sustainability (economic, social, ecological) or represents a systemically different approach. Examples include Fairtrade, organic agriculture or good manufacturing practice[8]

8 In some sustainability standards, environmental, social and animal-health issues are linked to or associated with quality parameters and requirements, such as in the GlobalGAP standard.

Guiding Element	Properties
	(b) one-dimensional: only social or environmental objective(s), only focused on product quality, the origin or a production region of product
Attribute	(a) product or product characteristics' focus (can be appreciated by consumer in end product)
	(b) processes and production methods (the so-called credence values, which the consumer cannot appreciate in the end product)
Scope	(a) vertical (focussing on all stages of the production and supply chain of a single product)
	(b) horizontal (focussing on management of a particular production or supply chain stage for several products)
Conformity assessment	(a) self-control or '(self-)declaration of conformity'
	(b) mutual control (second party verification)
	(c) independent control by a third party
	(d) third party conformity assessment, based on accreditation of certifying body and formal certification
Relational characterization	(a) Business to consumer (B2C)
	(b) Business to business (B2B)
	(c) NGO to consumer
Process of standard development	(a) Bottom-up (by producer and consumer associations, NGOs)[9]
	(b) Top-down (by industry organizations and by large companies)
	(c) Developed through the formal and non-formal standard systems[10]

9   Fairtrade, for instance, is half-owned by producer cooperatives; its standards and metrics are thus decided in large part by the representatives of farmers. Most voluntary standards for organic agriculture were also entirely or largely developed by farmers.

10 As already mentioned above, the formal standard system, comprising ISO, national and regional standard organizations, follow rather strict rules on transparency, openness and

Guiding Element	Properties
	(d) Multistakeholder process versus process with single or limited stakeholders

Some examples of VSS, created by different actors are:

By producers:	Fairtrade, various voluntary standards on organic agriculture, such as Demeter, Bioland, Naturland
By supermarkets:	GlobalGAP, British Retailer Consortium, Safe Quality Food
By processing companies:	Quality and Safety, Pro Planet, Filiéres Qualités, Mondelez's Coco Life
By ISO, national or regional standard organizations:[11]	ISO 14 000 on environmental management systems or ISO 22 000 on requirements for a food safety management system
Created by NGOs:	Marine Stewardship Council, Rainforest Alliance

Although at first sight standards and the above described quality infrastructure appear as simple technical specifications, few people actually think about standards as a social institution, their governance and how they can be used in the interest of some groups against others.[12] In other words, standards as an alternative mode of governance can also be tools of power and dominance. Mattli and Büthe contest the 'technical' nature of standards

scientific justification for standard development. This might not necessarily be the case for the non-formal standard-setting system.

11 National Standard Organizations in developed countries are mostly private, non-profit bodies, which deal with setting of pre-competitive standards for specific or several sectors. In contrast, most National Standard Organizations in developing countries are part of or associated with the government. Examples are the American National Standards Institute (ANSI) and the South African Bureau of Standards (SABS). As regards ISO, about 70 percent of national standard bodies participating in ISO activities are governmental (as communicated by R. Weissinger).

12 VSS may be misused or applied in a one-sided way, creating unilateral dependence particularly at the level of standard setting (because of intransparency or excessive stringency of requirements) and conformity assessment (through insistence on specific conformity assessment bodies and rigidity of applied testing protocols).

and underscore their 'political' role.[13] Lawrence Bush (2013) also argues that 'before embarking on making a standard, one should ask the central question: Is a standard the most appropriate form of governance in this particular situation? There are laws, regulations, statutes, customs, norms and habits that could perhaps be a better alternative'. Against this background, some critical questions for the characterization of a standard are (Joint Conference Church and Development, 2015):

- Who initiates and owns the standard and for whom is it made?
- Substance-wise, what does the standard manage or govern and what are its criteria and control points?
- What is the level of transparency in standard development and implementation and how can producers participate?
- What conformity assessment system is being applied and how transparent and participatory is its character?
- How is the legitimacy of the standard programme assured?
- How is the remuneration or benefit of participants in a standard programme guaranteed, in particular of producers?

In the past, one observed a trend in political discussions and policy positions in most developed countries that political measures targeting food quality, safety and related key environmental issues are most effective when they enhance efficiency of market forces rather than intervening directly. In other words, ethics and ecological consciousness became mostly privately managed issues.[14]

Tables 1 and 2 as well as Figure 2 provide an overview of the dynamics of covered acreage and production volume for those food products with the highest VSS-compliant market shares.

13 Mattli and Büthe (2003: 3–4) question: Do international standards benefit all or are there winners and losers, either in relative or absolute terms? What is the role of power and institutions in international disputes or bargains over standards? What defines power and how does it operate? First movers set the international standards agenda, and laggards, or second movers, pay the switching costs.

14 In 2010, the European Union adopted EU Best Practice Guidelines for Voluntary Certification Schemes for Agricultural Products and Foodstuffs (2010/C 341/04). The Guidelines however just frame best practice and do not justify governmental intervention.

Table 1: Production area of some VSS-certified commodities in 2018 and related growth rates[a]

Commodity	Minimum area certified (in thousand ha)	Share of global area (percentage)	Area growth 2017–2018 (percentage)	Area growth 2014–2018 (percentage)
Bananas	343	6.0	0.9	22.8
Cocoa	3,174	26.8	9.1	89.7
Coffee	2,196	20.7	–13.3	–12.2
Cotton	5,886	18.2	14.2	173.2
Oil palm	2,864	15.1	12.9	7.1
Soybeans	1,957	1.6	8.7	14.6
Sugarcane	1,947	7.4	–1.6	75.2
Tea	674	16.1	0.7	56.8
Total (based on minimum)	19,042	8.1	6.2	52.0
Total (based on maximum)	25,406	10.8	3.9	52.9
Total (based on average)	22,224	9.5	4.9	52.5

Note: The data in this table was not adjusted for multiple certification. So the minimum possible is reported. The total VSS-compliant area corresponds to the standard with the largest compliant area operating within a given sector by country.

a A recent study by Tayleur et al. (2018) that uses current spatial data for developing the first global map of VSS certification of seven commodity crops, synthesizing data from over one million farms to reveal the distribution of certification, comes (with the exclusion of organic certification for which spatial data were unavailable) to much lower figures for the share of certified crops in total production area than those provided in Table 1: coffee – 9 percent; cocoa and oil palm – 2.2 percent; tea – 2.0 percent; sugarcane – 0.6 percent; and soy – 0.2 percent.

Source: ITC, IISD, FiBL (2020: 3)

Table 2: Estimated minimum production volume of several VSS-certified agricultural commodities in 2018

Commodity	Estimated minimum production volume (in thousand MT)	Share of global production (percentage)	Production growth 2017–2018 (percentage)	Production growth 2014–2018 (percentage)
Bananas*	9,486	8.2	10.7	43.0
Cocoa	1,708	32.5	11.9	9.6
Coffee	2,660	25.8	–8.9	–15.1
Soybeans	6,161	1.8	18.4	80.3
Tea	1,398	22.1	9.6	61.4

* Production volume of bananas for Global G.A.P. is missing.

Note: The data in this tables was not adjusted for multiple certification. So the minimum possible is reported. The total VSS-compliant area corresponds to the standard with the largest compliant area operating within a given sector by country.

Source: ITC, IISD, FiBL (2020: 5)

Figure 2: Evolution of estimated minimum production area for selected VSS-certified food commodities for the period 2008–2018

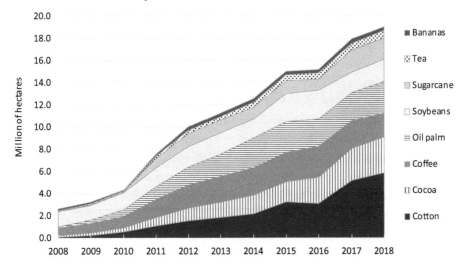

Note: The products are sorted by area. For the purpose of the figure, it is assumed that a maximum amount of multiple certification is occurring within each commodity and the minimum possible VSS-compliant area is shown. This corresponds to the standards with the largest compliant area operating within a given sector.

Source: ITC, IISD, FiBL, (2020: 4)

What do Tables 1 and 2, as well as Figure 2 leave us with? For a number of food commodities and beverages, VSS are no longer a novelty phenomenon serving niche markets. Over the past decade and more, they have increasingly found their way into mainstream export markets. For some exported products, VSS have de facto become a license to operate. The recent market context shows continued growth, an expanding share of agricultural land, which surpasses the 20 percent mark in some commodities destined for export, and a dominance of single-sector standards (ITC, FiBL, IISD, 2019: IX). As will however be shown later, despite such high and still rising market shares of VSS-compliant products the VSS transformation record has generally been disappointing. As will in particular be illustrated for the case of cocoa, although about one third of global cocoa production volume is estimated to be VSS-certified, cocoa production is far from sustainable and rural poverty remains alarming.

To avoid any misunderstanding though, often the claim is made by advocates of 'modern' (external-input-intensive, factory-like) agriculture that only VSS-certified agriculture would be sustainable. However, estimates suggest that around 5 million farmers participate in VSS schemes, currently representing not more than approximately 1 percent of global agricultural land, 1 percent of all farmers and 2 percent of agricultural production (Buntzel and Mari, 2016: 297). There are however many other production methods, for instance agro-ecological or agro-forestry ones, which are also qualifying as sustainable and particularly suited to small-scale farming.

There are many different kinds of VSS, and the distinctions between them are not always clear. By definition, all sustainability standards are designed to contribute to 'sustainability', but they aim to do so in different ways. It is not necessarily the case that they will be treated identically in relation to national or international trade rules, or will have the same impact in terms of achieving public policy objectives. It is worth being aware of the differences, as criticisms of one type of VSS may not apply to all. Different kinds of standards may be appropriate for different purposes, or in different circumstances. In discussions, it is thus necessary to be specific about the kind of standard that is being referred to, and to determine the characteristics of this particular standard, before deciding if it is suitable or unsuitable for a particular purpose.

There has been considerable debate as to whether VSS should really be thought of as opportunity for development. It is clear that they should create additional value in a supply chain, but it is equally clear that they would be expected to result in additional costs. If some producers are able to expand their market share by meeting VSS, it is likely that the market share of others may shrink. Which participants in the supply chain capture any available increase in value? How are the costs and benefits distributed at different points along the supply chain? Which participants are most likely to benefit and whether others might also lose out from the introduction of standards? All these critical issues are uncertain and we will elaborate on some of them below.

As will be analysed in much more detail below, claiming sustainability off the back of a certification system is misleading. Although the terms 'certified commodity or product' and 'sustainable commodity or product' are still often – wrongly – used interchangeably, 'certified' cannot be claimed to be 'sustainable' merely on the basis of certification, no matter what VSS is concerned (Fountain and Huetz-Adams, 2020b: 34).

B. The Ambivalent Antecedents of Voluntary Sustainability Standards (VSS)

Although a number of VSS emerged well before the late 1980s,[15] many of them were launched in the period between the mid-1980s and the turn of the century. This was a pivotal conjuncture, in which rising public ecological consciousness and pressure for greening policy and economic activity came to be framed in terms of individual choice and morally responsible decision-making, for it was the breakthrough period of both the green movement and neoliberal ideology (Dale, 2011).

On the one hand, the international concern and debate on pressing global environmental problems intensified, related to the land-mark first report of the Club of Rome on 'The Limits to Growth', large leaps of oil prices in the 1970s and 1980s and an increasing concern about the looming dangers resulting from climate change and biodiversity loss. The United Nations Conference on Environment and Development (UNCED), also known as the Earth Summit, was held in Rio de Janeiro in early June 1992. An important achievement of the summit was the agreement on creating the Climate Change Convention and the Convention on Biological Diversity. UNCED also adopted the Rio Declaration on Environment and Development and Agenda 21. UNCED undoubtedly

---

15 The concepts of organic agriculture, for instance, were developed at the beginning of the twentieth century by Sir Albert Howard, F.H. King, Rudolf Steiner and others. The Demeter Biodynamic Certification program was established in 1928, and as such was the first ecological label for organically produced food.

established the concept of sustainability firmly on national and international political and economic agendas. In implementing the Rio Declaration and Agenda 21, however, it became evident that the projections and warnings of the authors of 'The Limits to Growth' would require some rather drastic public intervention, challenging the growth paradigm, in order to make economic, social and ecological sustainability a reality. Against this very background, various circles in Western countries advanced the concept of 'public-private partnerships' that should jointly with and supported by governmental regulation and initiatives implement Agenda 21 in a sort of co-governance system, involving the private sector, civil society organizations and governments.[16]

VSS became one of these tools and part of the partnerships. People's despair with political inaction or inefficiency gave rise to the ethical consumer movement, premised on the idea that private purchasing decisions might determine what kind of society we live in (i.e. green consumerism). It rests on the insight that production and consumption structures have to change simultaneously; otherwise either sides' endeavours soon face a dead end. It was also felt that VSS might overcome public regulatory limits and inertia[17] and be a smooth steering instrument for making globalization and associated international supply chains more sustainable and fairer.

On the other hand, since the mid-1980s neoliberalism gained the upper hand among policy makers in developed countries. It linked individual, mostly economic liberty with deregulation of governmental interventions into market forces (both nationally and internationally) and individual consumerism, yielding the tenets that identity and subjectivity are defined in terms of what we consume. It was emphasized that 'free markets' empower the consumer, and that corporate behaviour is driven by consumer choice (see Box 3 on green consumerism).

---

16 Public Private Partnerships represent cooperative arrangements and initiatives between a public and private entities, partly also involving civil society, that use the financial resources of the private sector and the mobilization power of NGOs to carry out the legal activities or functions of the public sector.

17 The Agreement on Technical Barriers to Trade (TBT) of the 1995-created World Trade Organization provides the framework for the use of government regulation and technical requirements (the latter being standards in WTO parlance). It has however remained a contentious issue whether not only product-characteristics-related standards but also non-product-related standards on processes and production methods, which deal with environmental and social issues, are subject to WTO disciplines. This has led to inertia among governments to pro-actively use standards for influencing the so-called 'credence' values of products (i.e. social and ecological production characteristics that a consumer cannot appreciate or judge on face value).

As conceptually well framed by Samanth Subramanian referring to Fairtrade standards, VSS

> cemented the notion that the modern corporation would be ethical if only someone held up a lamp and showed it the way. Capitalism did not have to be feared; the market would figure out its own checks and balances, through labelling agencies such as Fairtrade and Rainforest Alliance, without having to be regulated by any higher authority. Persistent and egregious inequality could be solved by deft pleats and tucks to the garb of trade, rather than by a full reconsideration of its fabric and seams. (Subramanian, 2019)

Box 3: Green consumerism: Can we really shop our way to a better world?

When eco-labels emerged in large number in the 1990s it was argued that green consumer issues would inspire a growing number of people to critically examine their own lifestyles. Green consumerism would provide an incentive to businesses to clean up their act, empower individuals to accept personal responsibility for their own choices, and would also be supportive to campaigns of social organizations on more sustainability.

The plea for the 'power of sustainable consumption' however overestimates the real power of consumers. As global production conditions are far too complex, information on the supply chain and real sustainability impact too nebulous, as well as alternatives rare or not available at all, consumers may find it difficult to really buy more sustainably.[18] As a result consumers are unclear about the criteria, by which 'greenness' is defined, and about the sources of reliable information and can therefore be fooled.

There is also a debate that pits 'liberal consumerists' against 'counterconsumerism'. Whereas for the former the environmental crisis results are linked to the quality of consumption, for the latter it is also imperative to go beyond the quality perspective and consume less in quantity.

Umair Muhammad (2016) in his book on social activism in the age of individualism argues that voting with our wallets on consumption tends to only

---

18 By way of illustration, it is very difficult for a consumer to decide whether and when a locally grown apple is more sustainable after taking production, transport and cold storage into account, compared to an apple produced in and shipped from overseas (e.g. from New Zealand, Chile or South Africa). Similarly, should one choose the factory-farmed local chicken or its free-range, organically-fed cousin, air-freighted from abroad?

make token changes in consumers' lives. When faced with this kind of critique, lifestyle-centric activists often counter that conscious consumerism is a good 'first step'. In his experience, however, those who endorse the idea that better consumption is a form of activism have a hard time moving on to anything else. Year after year he has seen those engaged in promoting lifestyle changes remain stuck in place. Their objective has become to convince more and more individuals to become vegetarians, purchase Fairtrade coffee, carpool to work, etc. Moreover, for most of those who sign on to this approach, the only 'next step' they seem inclined to take is to intensify their engagement with conscious consumerism. It seems to him that there is a qualitative difference between, on the one hand, embracing the individualism that defines lifestyle-centric activism and, on the other, coming to recognize the social dimension of the problems we face. The former is not a bridge to the latter, but a distraction away from it.

Green consumerism distracts from the very need for public regulation and mandatory rules for controlling long international supply chains. It is a myth that consumers can play the role of national policy. What is rather required is a systemic change moving away from the take-make-dispose model of economic growth to a model restorative and regenerative by nature. Bearing in mind the different purchasing power and importance given to economic versus environmental considerations by consumers in developed and developing countries, individual purchasing decisions can help, up to a certain level, avoid or alleviate excessive consumption implications. Lasting changes towards true sustainability or transformational change, however, require structural changes in policy, incentive systems and economic structures (e.g. organic standards per se are insufficient to transform agriculture – see below for further detail).

As Rundgren (2015: 286) aptly put, the discourse on green consumerism 'is disconnected from the realities of farming, and the factors that determine farmers' choices'.

The outsourcing pressure of labor and resource-intensive industries, the so-called de-territorialization, gained more and more momentum and in its wake the concept of international supply or value chains emerged against the background of the curtailment of the state as economic agent and regulator. Supply chain governance became an important issue and quite a number of VSS, in particular business-to-business (B2B) standards were architectured to play that role. Governments disengaged from the regulation of ethical and ecological aspects of production and confined its focus to core food safety issues – managing ethical and ecological issues became a private and business-level governance issue (see also Göpel, 2020: 149).

In the global agro-food sector, a profound transformation took place in the context of the industrialization and globalization of agriculture, based on a very external-input-intensive and highly specialized mass-production model. As a result, few globally active companies control the world seed, fertilizer, agro-chemical, and food processing markets. Large supermarkets have most of food retail in their grip. All these actors wield enormous power in international supply chains and tend to use VSS for quality and environmental risk management (for more information, see IPES-Food, 2017).

The transformation of the global agro-food sector and its supply chain structure resulted in:

- A consolidation of the supply chains leading to a few companies that control one or several stages of the supply chain, notably in trade, processing and retail;
- The cutting out of middlemen and wholesale trade in international food marketing by direct purchasing arrangements of large supermarket groups;
- Drastic reduction of the number of producers and suppliers through the selection and designation of 'dedicated suppliers' that are very much dependent on the retailers[19];
- Use of certain rather strict B2B VSS focused on product quality and food safety, with supplementary control points on ecological and social issue.[20]

As a result and also in the light of the limits of public governance over international supply chains, such VSS have become an effective private governance system for global value chains linking supply-chain members across many borders, who are however dependent on the large buyers in a unilateral way.

A third factor that spawned VSS was the fierce global competition in the 'commodified' food markets. Conventional food markets are mostly mass markets of anonymous commodities. Growth rates of sales in conventional food markets have declined over time as a result of saturation of demand in most

---

19 This included pressure on small-scale producers and smallholder farmers and their cooperatives to compete in the supply chains or get left out.
20 In the GlobalGAP standard, for instance, environmental issues are in fact related to the highest number of total control points. However, most of these particular environmental issues are primarily related to assuring food safety.

developed countries. Consumer spending on food has seen sluggish growth in recent decades,[21] whereas VSS-compliant food production and sales have often recorded double digit growth rates in the developed world. VSS and related eco-labels have therefore increasingly been used for market differentiation between certified products with specific credence characteristics from other products in the mass market. As will be highlighted later, there is also evidence that supermarkets realized higher sales' margins from VSS-compliant food relative to the conventional one. This said, however, as will also be analysed later, the more successful a standard and label is and the higher its market share, the less value it has as differentiating characteristic in a competitive market (Rundgren, 2011a).

A fourth factor that put its stamp on emerging VSS was the BSE epidemic that emerged in the UK in the mid-1980s and reigned in Europe and (spread through trade) to a few other regions till the late 1990s.[22] It was one of the biggest global food scares in history and led to the introduction of due diligence requirements for food producers, handlers and sellers. Faced with the BSE epidemic, the UK issued a Food Safety Act in 1990. Under this Act, due diligence defence is the primary way to prevent legal repercussions if there is a food safety incident at business level. It is designed to balance the protection of the consumer against defective food with the right of traders, so that they won't be convicted of something they took all reasonable care to prevent.

The Food Safety Act states that a business has a due diligence defence if reasonable checks of the food were carried out in all the circumstances or it was reasonable to rely on checks carried out by the company who supplied the food.

The due diligence requirements were reflected and incorporated in many food-related VSS, most prominently under the concept of Hazard Analysis and

---

21 In the United States, for instance, inflation-adjusted growth of food sales in grocery stores (excluding convenience stores) averaged 1.39 percent per year for the period 2010 to 2017, compared with –0.05 percent per year from 2000 to 2009 (grocery stores account for over 90 percent of all US food store sales). See: www.ers.usda.gov/topics/food-markets-prices/retailing-wholesaling/retail-trends.aspx

22 BSE is the acronym for Bovine Spongiform Encephalopathy, sometimes also called mad cow disease, because its symptoms usually include aggression and a lack of coordination. The disease infects cows and attacks their central nervous system. It is usually fatal. Spread to humans is believed to result in variant Creutzfeldt–Jakob disease. BSE was the result of an infection by a misfolded protein, known as a prion. Cattle are believed to have been infected by being fed meat-and-bone meal, which contained the remains of cattle who spontaneously developed the disease or scrapie-infected sheep products. To prevent the disease, a ban on feeding meat and bone meal to cattle was introduced in Europe. In disease-free countries, import controls, feeding regulations and surveillance measures were introduced or reinforced (Ainsworth and Carrington, 2000).

Critical Control Points (HACCP). This concept and related approaches found their way into Regulation (EC) No 852/2004 of the European Union on the hygiene of foodstuffs and the later development of the ISO 22000 Standard on food safety management systems, adopted in 2011.[23] The HACCP system has thus become a sort of 'enforced self-regulation' (Buntzel and Mari, 2016: 64).

It should however not go without comment that despite due diligence requirements and HACCP approaches being incorporated in many food-related VSS, food scares have continued to resurface, mostly as a result of insufficient economic sustainability of producers and the related cost-treadmill.[24]

To sum up, VSS have emerged as part of several converging trends in the last two decades of the twentieth century, including:

- emphasizing the market and consumer choice as important tools to accomplish ethical, environmental, social and economic goals;
- facilitating government de-regulation, which leaves more self-regulation to the private sector[25];
- holding those that bring products to the market accountable for the safety of their food products, a responsibility that extends to the suppliers of the products, and their suppliers in turn;
- the emergence of a system that leads to so-called value chains where each link is taken care of by independent companies that are under the constant threat of being replaced, permanently competing with others;

23 HACCP is a systematic preventive approach to food safety from biological, chemical, physical and more recently radiological hazards in production processes that can cause the finished product to be unsafe and designs measures to reduce these risks to a safe level. HACCP attempts to avoid hazards rather than attempting to inspect finished products for the effects of those hazards. HACCP now is extended to all sectors and stages of the food industry, going into meat, poultry, seafood, dairy, and has spread from the farm to the fork. HACCP encompasses the following seven principles: (i) conduct a hazard analysis; (ii) identify critical control points; (iii) establish critical limits for each critical control point; (iv) establish critical control point monitoring requirements; (v) devise corrective actions; (vi) create procedures for ensuring that the HACCP system is working as intended; and (vii) establish record keeping procedures (for more information see www.haccpalliance.org/sub/index.html).

24 Due diligence requirements for food safety, notably in the context of B2B VSS have certainly improved food safety in recent year. However, they have not been sufficient to arrest the growth of food-borne diseases and food scares. For more information in this regard see Siegner (2019).

25 In fact, real government regulation on sustainability issues did not exist and with emerging VSS governments gave up any intention of proper regulation.

- introducing a stiff global competition that makes differentiation in the market place an essential survival strategy to escape 'commodity hell' (see also Rundgren, 2017).

C. Opportunities and Benefits that Could Arise from VSS

When reviewing the pros, but later also the cons of VSS, one should bear in mind that five key thematic clusters are sort of intermingled in the VSS edifice: (i) the transformational change potential of these standards; (ii) the interplay between standards and trade governance issues; (iii) the macro-economic development impact of VSS on structural, social and ecological issues; (iv) the business-level impact (meso and supply-chain related) on innovation, product quality, productivity and competitiveness; and (v) the awareness-building role for producers and consumers. One should also bear in mind that VSS impacts can arise at enterprise, local/regional, national and international level. Investment in and efforts made for VSS implementation and certification by a particular producer might therefore not have direct proportional effects and impact at company level. Parts or even most of the benefits might arise elsewhere at regional, national or international level.[26]

To begin with, VSS have undoubtedly created new markets (such as with less environmental load, e.g. chlorine-free paper or agro-chemical free food or with better social conditions, e.g. without child labour or respecting minimum wage requirements). As will be highlighted later, it must however be doubted that through such schemes VSS can play a transformational role and bring about a system-level change within the concept of a green economy.

VSS are also tools that may encourage improvements in efficiency, productivity,[27] innovation, product quality and a desirable shift in production and consumption patterns. However, most of the related costs and investment for such

---

26 By way of illustration, climate-change mitigation efforts at farm level may improve soil quality for the concerned farmer, but these efforts will also bear on reduced national and global GHG emissions.

27 As will be emphasized below, 'productivity' should not be confined to 'return or yield in commercial terms'. A major challenge in boosting productivity is to do it sustainably and not based on 'resource-mining'. There is also the need to redefine productivity as 'integral productivity', which integrates economic with social, cultural and ecological components.

improvements are shouldered by producers and public donors (either directly or indirectly through NGOs).[28] Moreover, efficiency gains, productivity and quality improvements do not necessarily strengthen the economic sustainability of most producers, because quality price premiums and producer costs suffer from the cost-treadmill effect (see Box 5). To materialize efficiency, productivity and quality improvements, shifts in production patterns as well as innovation impulses at company level for VSS-compliant production also often require or are impossible without government investment in technical infra-structure (e.g. roads and other transport facilities, telecom), institutions (e.g. accredited testing laboratories, accreditation bodies) or extension services. Such government support competes in most developing countries with or runs the risk of crowding out public investment and flanking support in other more urgent development and social issues, including market improvement for the informal sector. Conversely, in most developed countries VSS-triggered quality and productivity improvements have stood on the shoulders of massive public agricultural support programs.[29]

VSS can also be a tool for some internalization of environmental and (to a much lesser extent) social externalities. This said, however, such cost internalization has mostly been lopsided. On the one hand, power asymmetry along supply chains limits the scope for internalization at producer level, if any, because of the cost-treadmill trap. On the other hand, higher production costs and price premiums dampen consumer demand for sustainable products, such as organic food, as conventional food product prices remain unduly low, because of perverse direct and indirect subsidies and the absent sanctioning of environmental and social damage.[30]

As already mentioned above, sustainability standards should not be a substitute for public regulation and enforcement of basic social and environmental requirements. VSS may however contain requirements that go beyond legal

---

28 According to an ITC/EUI study (2016), it is estimated that producers alone bear up to some 65 percent of VSS implementation costs and about 55 percent of certification costs.

29 In most developed countries public support has accounted for 40–60 percent of farmers' revenues in recent years. Meanwhile, public support measures falling under the 'Green Box' of the WTO Agreement on Agriculture account for 80–90 percent of all public support to agriculture. This puts farmers, who participate in VSS programmes at a huge competitive advantage, relative to producers in developing countries (see Hepburn and Bellmann, 2014).

30 Social damage concerns, for instance, the employment of ill-paid or child labour, excessive working hours or insufficient occupational safety, to name but a few issues.

requirements. VSS may also drive and serve as a reference point for new or extended governmental regulation.

VSS often either explicitly or implicitly lead to improved managerial, organizational and accounting practices of producers or producer groups, resulting from training and advice as well as investment in extension. Based on a large number of country and commodity field assessment studies, researchers of the International Centre for Integrated Assessment and Sustainable Development at the University of Maastricht in the Netherlands come to the conclusion that these indirect, capacity-building benefits and the resulting awareness raising on sustainability issues is the most important effect of VSS and not turning the market around (Glasbergen, 2018: 250).

According to Rundgren (2017), in general, VSS are not particularly efficient in dealing with problems that are rooted in fundamental structures of society, the market or the economy. They do normally work well when they are about a simple substitution of a technology, e.g. chlorine-free paper or GMO-free food. Fundamental or systemic problems can – and should – be accomplished by mandatory regulation. VSS can then supplement regulatory requirements or even go beyond those. By way of illustration, a fundamental transformation towards genuinely sustainable agriculture must be based on a number of regulatory and fiscal policy measures that sanction or discourage undesirable practices and reward the generation of socially desirable public goods and services (i.e. clean ground water, attractive landscapes, biodiversity preservation, diversity of production patterns, climate change mitigation, to name but a few). This would also include regulation on organic agriculture; VSS on organic agriculture could supplement these policy measures. They are, at the moment, however no substitute for regulation as it paves the way for first stone in constructing a sustainable world (see also Hoffmann, 2011, 2013).

If VSS are couched within frameworks of cooperative and fair production and marketing, e.g. in the context of community-supported agriculture, cooperative marketing boards etc. VSS may well become a constituent tool for new and much more just market relations, including fairer international trade. However, recent trends in the marketing structure seem to contradict such claims and opportunities. Whereas in 2009 every second consumer bought Fairtrade products in special 'world shops' in Germany, which offer better terms to producers, in 2017 only every 10th consumer used these shops, buying most Fairtrade goods in supermarkets (according to information from Forum Fairer Handel, Datenblatt Fairer Handel, 2019).

Before concluding this section one should also recall that VSS form a complementary element that reflects new challenges and dynamics in markets at a time of static TBT and SPS rules[31] as well as slowly advancing national regulation. National and international debates on environmental issues and pressures loomed high in the 1990s and 2000s, but this contrasted with the impression of lethargy, insufficient or no action in national regulation. Strengthened by the evolving debate on the Sustainable Development Goals, VSS became a dynamic tool of NGOs and the private sector to frame requirements for less problematic environmental and social production methods, both at national and international level. VSS became one of the firm pillars that underpinned and strengthened the belief that green consumerism can change the world.

D. The Impact of VSS and the Insufficient Leverage for Transformational Change

According to the emergent critical mass of research on impact assessment of VSS and related sustainability standard theories of change,

> sustainability standards alone will not be able to deliver the scale and depth of impacts required to lift millions of smallholders and workers from poverty, nor deliver on environmental, inequality, climate change and employment challenges. While there is ample evidence ... that sustainability standards unlock benefits for workers, producers, their organisations, communities and environments, it is rarely the case that they have a transformational poverty impact. (Nelson and Martin, 2013: 104)

A recent study of the Changing Markets Foundation on VSS impact in palm oil and textiles production as well as fisheries concludes that the certification schemes in these sectors

> often provide cover for environmental destruction and human rights violations ... Despite good intentions, these schemes have lost their way and have – in the

---

31 As already highlighted in Box 1, the WTO SPS Committee debated VSS under the title 'private standards' between mid-2005 and early 2011. The discussion on whether such VSS should fall under the (rather strict) regulatory disciplines of the SPS Agreement remained however inconclusive (see www.wto.org/english/news_e/news11_e/sps_30mar11_e.htm).

best case – only modestly contributed to slowing environmental destruction or improving companies' sustainability performance. The proliferation of palm oil certification has not stopped the clearance of forests or draining of peatlands; certification of sustainable fisheries has not slowed down the collapse of fish stocks; and the textile industry continues to be one of the most polluting and rapidly growing sectors on the planet, despite the existence of over 100 sustainability initiatives seeking to put it on a more sustainable track. (Changing Markets Foundation, 2018: 85)[32]

The same conclusion is drawn in a study by Murphy-Bokern and Kleemann (2015: 21), which reviews the use of Corporate Social Responsibility schemes and related VSS for reducing greenhouse gas emissions in the food sector. According to the authors,

the great majority of firms are focused on incremental product or process improvement . . .. Strategies that support radical change are confined largely to companies in niche areas, particularly those associated with the organic sector . . .. Thus, tipping point change with large-scale emission reduction cannot be expected from firms' existing Corporate Responsibility strategies.[33]

Turning to the 'so-called' great benefits to producers for using VSS, an in-depth study of the Committee on Sustainability Assessment (COSA) on VSS impacts (COSA, 2013: 41, figure 5.4.), which focused on coffee and cocoa farmers in twelve countries covering the period 2009–2013, showed that net household

---

32 For the case of the Better Cotton Initiative (BCI), for instance, the study states: 'To tout the BCI certificate as a guarantee of sustainability is misleading. BCI certification only means 'better' if not-certified farms do not meet any international or national regulations and laws at all . . . The extremely rapid growth of BCI, in spite of its clear shortcomings, raises serious concerns about the future of sustainable cotton. With its support for GM cotton and tolerance of pesticide use, the BCI is failing to promote cotton that is truly better for the environment and to protect the health of cotton growers. In fact, it appears to be crowding out and restricting the growth potential of more sustainable schemes, such as GOTS (Global Organic Textile Standard), and there is a real risk the cotton market could suffer as a result' (Changing Markets Foundation, 2018: 76 and 78).

33 Glasbergen (2018) reaches the same conclusion. He stresses that 'for a social and environmental benefit to be achieved in agriculture, a more structural or drastic change is ultimately required: certifications and voluntary standards alone cannot achieve the expected outcomes'. The South Center has recently commissioned the preparation of a model Green Investment Treaty, which also emphasizes this point (see: http://stockholmtreatylab.org/wp-content/uploads/2018/10/The-Green-Investment-Treaty-with-author-info.pdf, part III on Responsible Investment and Environmental Transparency).

Figure 3: VSS impact assessment results for cocoa and coffee producers in 12 developing countries (comparing certified with conventional farmers, and reflecting the variation), 2009–2013

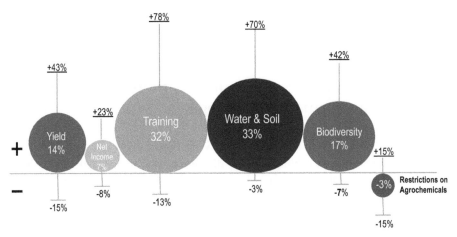

income only increased by 7 percent and yield by 14 percent when certified producers are compared to uncertified producers (see Figure 3). Productivity increases and decreasing prices are inherent characteristics of the current system since only in this way certified products can compete with conventional products in the market and may thus increase their sales; and larger producers are in a better position to achieve this. In this context it also has to be noted that productivity increases of (often large-scale) farmers under certification schemes, which have a correlation with income increases through higher yields, will lead to lower prices for certified products in the long run. This has in particular a bearing on producers who wish to newly enter certification and related supply chains due to the additional difficulty or prevention of entry through lower margins or premiums that cannot cover upfront VSS adjustment costs and later ongoing certification costs.

According to the first global COSA report (COSA, 2013: 53 and figure 5.19), the most significant impacts of certification were identified in the areas of training (pertaining to good agricultural practices, improving farm operations, record keeping, environmental resource management, health and social issues, marketing and financial literacy skills),[34] followed by water preservation and quality

34 As highlighted earlier, according to ISO Standards and Guides on conformity assessment capacity building should not be part of the certification process itself. It is worthwhile mentioning that almost all such projects are funded by development agencies or alike and that there are few – if any – studies comparing similar interventions with or without VSS certification.

improvement, soil conservation and improvement of soil health and biodiversity conservation and protection (in particular plant diversity and tree density) (COSA, 2013: 60, table 5.3). While not being of direct significance for farmer livelihoods, these factors might nevertheless contribute to the improvement of living conditions in the long term and through indirect pathways.[35]

Box 4: Impact assessment of VSS: Incremental versus transformational change

Depending on the focus of the concerned VSS, the impact may be limited to one or a small number of sustainability issues or dimensions (e.g. some social conditions, occupational safety, deforestation, reduced fertilizer and agro-chemical use etc.) or be multi-dimensional (see figure below).

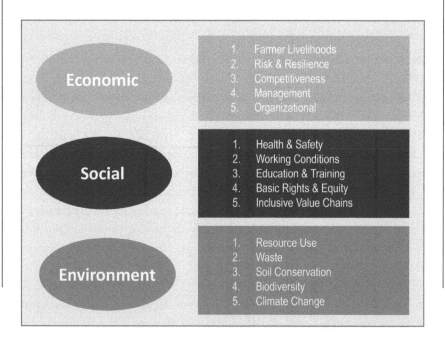

Therefore, conceptually the effectiveness of the impact of VSS can be measured differently. On the one hand, effectiveness can be evaluated on the basis of achieving

35 For example, the case of Farmer Field Schools for smallholder tea producers in Kenya shows the potential for increasing average yield and income diversification through training (Waarts, 2014).

individually set goals (i.e. incrementally improving certain aspects of sustainability, which may be particularly important for consumers or corporate buyers). On the other hand, individual multidimensional VSS and VSS taken collectively should also contribute to transformational change, which is much required in global agriculture. This concerns agro-ecological intensification, much-reduced resource and external input use, structural change, in particular the reduction of industrial livestock production, the promotion of rural livelihoods, enhancing the resilience of agriculture, and the promotion of sustainable and resilient food systems, including processing, transportation and consumption.

There are cases, where VSS focusing on individually set goals may contradict much-required transformational change. By way of illustration, VSS-compliant production of protein-rich crops for concentrate animal feed production (including fish-farming), such as soy, can prevent deforestation, optimize agro-chemical use and encourage intercropping of soy. This, however, does not alter the more systemic problem of industrial livestock and fish-farming production, for which protein-rich concentrate feed is an essential element. Industrial livestock production is the environmental hotspot of agricultural production as regards greenhouse gas emissions, nitrogen overuse and dumping of liquid manure and related groundwater contamination.

The same ambivalence may occur between the impacts of VSS at the micro- and macro-economic level. By way of illustration, certain VSS might overcome the problem of child labour at the company level. This may however lead to the occurrence of family-related poverty problems at the regional or macro-economic level either temporarily or permanently. Therefore, it would be misleading to simply aggregate the company-level impact of VSS and combine data of several firms and take them as synonymous for macro-economic effects.[36]

Neghi et al. (2020: 218) also emphasize that 'those farmers that can afford certification may even cause more environmental damage by enlarging their cultivated area, which stands in contradiction to the general purpose of VSS (and at the same time proves that VSS cannot prevent over-production/consumption)'.

As already mentioned above, it is important not to overlook that the costs and benefits of VSS use might arise at different points and levels. Those bearing a

---

36 According to the analysis of Schader et al. (2014), the sustainability assessment approaches to food the authors reviewed 'mix the social and the business perspectives of sustainability and do often not consciously distinguish between them. The two perspectives . . .. can employ the same impact categories or indicators. For instance, protecting soil and water resources is beneficial to both the individual farm and the society. Whether the operation of a single farm can be sustained is of "private business interest," but the operational sustainability of the single farm might not necessarily be of "societal interest". Thus, the business perspective does not always correlate with the sustainability of a society'.

significant part of the costs might not necessarily earn a commensurate share of the benefits of VSS compliance.

In sum, it is safe to say that there is a severe lack of information and analysis, including appropriate methodologies and a sufficient stock of data, on sustainability impact assessment in the context of VSS use. Currently, it is estimated that for food systems alone some 30–40 sustainability assessment programs exist that regularly publish results.[37]

Funding support to some of these impact assessment programs does not seem to be unbiased from both the public and private side, methodological approaches differ, data used for the impact assessment is often not made publically accessible, and the interpretation of impact assessment results is not following uniform rules. Against this background, the UN Forum on Sustainability Standards (UNFSS) had proposed to form a working group on sustainability impact assessment to address these shortcomings, contradictions and conceptual challenges (for more information, see Hoffmann and Grothaus, 2015).

Source for figure: Giovannucci (2014)

The term 'sustainability standards' is generally loosely defined, so that almost any management approach and technology can accommodate it, as and when required by supply chain managers. Many VSS focus on exported cash crops (which often are the former 'colonial' crops) that almost exclusively represent mono-crops. By the very definition, a mono-crop, in particular when planted at large scale, is anything but truly sustainable for agriculture.[38] Therefore, many of the concerned VSS deal with limiting or managing the environmental and social damage caused by large-scale mono-crops,[39] rather than making agricultural

---

37 A considerable part of them is primarily used for research, others for policy advice, producer monitoring, self-monitoring, for certification, for consumer information and landscape planning (for an overview of existing food-related sustainability assessment programs, see Schader et al., 2014). For the comparison of impact assessment approaches it is necessary to review methodological questions of the scope of sustainability assessment approaches (i.e. primary purpose, level of assessment, geographical, sector and thematic scope as well as the perspectives on sustainability), the precision of the approaches, the assessment results and their interpretation.

38 Multifunctional agro-ecosystems should be designed to be both sustained by nature and sustainable in their nature. They should guarantee the reproductive function and capacity of the concerned agro-ecological system (Tittonell, 2014: 53).

39 For instance, bananas, coffee, cocoa, tea, pineapple, soy, cotton, palm oil or maize/corn, to name but the most important.

production truly sustainable. This, of course, limits the potential of the standards to contribute to the much-required fundamental transformation of agriculture, which would have to be largely based on mosaics of highly diversified, integrated (i.e. combining crop production and animal husbandry) and largely autonomous (closed nutrient-cycle-based), knowledge and labour-intensive agro-ecological production systems, in which smallholders play a pivotal role both for environmental and social sustainability.[40]

Although there is a rising number of multi-issue or multi-dimensional VSS many are still dealing with one or only a few issues, such as safe use of agrochemicals or proper labour rights. This runs the risk of horizontal problem shifting as more attention is given to the easier to deliver benefits. In some cases, because of crowding out of financial and managerial capacity for standard compliance or the one-sided focus of VSS, by plugging one hole VSS may create two or more others.[41] This raises the issue of the holistic and cross-cutting nature of the sustainability impact of VSS.

According to the study of Nelson and Martin (2013: 88), 'there are also thematic areas where sustainability standards are not tackling poverty or broader sustainability issues adequately as part of their required standards – e.g. greenhouse gas emissions and climate change adaptation, gender issues, and living wage'. Without the adequate tackling of some key structural or socio-economic issues, such as insecure land tenure, gender equality or access to adequate finance, VSS are unlikely to harness their full potential or remain limited to 'better-developed and manageable exclaves'.

Also, many VSS do not specify the result the standard requirements and related control points shall achieve, but they focus on the company-level instruments that shall be applied to achieve the standard objective. In this way, VSS try to make sustainability practicable at a company level, but run the risk that VSS implementation and not the resulting sustainability impact becomes an end in

---

40 Such smaller production units not only have a higher productivity of the entire production system (not an individual crop), but also a higher profitability, because of the low-external-input dependence. For more information, see UNCTAD (2013).

41 Prominent examples in this regard are VSS for biofuels and concentrate animal feed. The hype of biofuels, for instance, has boosted land prices and land speculation in several countries. Among other things, this has put tremendous pressure on the profitability of agriculture, including organic production. Organic producers have consequently found it increasingly difficult to expand their cropping area and, in some countries, the area under organic production decreased although demand for organic products kept increasing.

itself, thus confusing means and end. In his book The Audit Society: Rituals of Verification, Michael Power (1999) argues that 'the audit explosion is driven by vested interest and a failed attempt to minimize risk by focusing systems rather than actual performance'. In fact, the widespread emergence of VSS has fuelled the growth of a standard setting, auditing and certification edifice, which has de facto become a lucrative commercial service sector with vested interests, which right from the outset has also involved or attracted a good number of NGOs, for some of which such activities have become a lucrative source of funding.

In an ISEAL review seeking the opinions of 100 'thought-leaders' on VSS on what creates trust in a standard system, respondents gave the following rating:

- 55 percent thought that the verification process, including accreditation and third-party certification was important,
- 38 percent singled out a standard document at just the right level (science-based, comprehensive, and practical),
- 35 percent pointed to a credible multi-stakeholder standard-setting process that has the support from all relevant parties (producers, NGOs, companies),
- 32 percent accorded priority to a transparent governance model, and
- only 11 percent of respondents pointed to the importance of showing impact.[42]

Commenting on these results, Gunnar Rundgren (a former IFOAM President and initiator of the eco-label KRAV in Sweden) found them very discouraging. In his view the people involved in the 'sustainability industry' (folks that are part of the environmental movement, CSR managers, employees of certification and standardization bodies, consultants like himself, international NGOs or international organizations) are losing the grip of what is important – the impact (Rundgren, 2011b). Similar criticism is voiced by Sina Trinkwalder (2016), an entrepreneur in fair-produced and traded clothing in Germany, who characterizes such tendencies as 'modern trade in indulgences'.

When discussing issues of VSS impact assessment it is therefore of vital importance that one does not confine the analysis and debate to optimizing the process of VSS implementation and certification. This points to shortcomings in the system of certification: it verifies whether the concerned production practices

---

42 Respondents had the option of multiple answers; this is why percentages do not add up to 100 percent (ISEAL Alliance, 2011).

are in conformity with the VSS requirements, but does not tell us anything about the validity of the claim, nor whether the conformity really improves true sustainability of producers and societal sustainability. VSS implementation and impact need to be evaluated in the context of their usefulness and concrete contribution to moving to truly sustainable agriculture that also improves the livelihood of farmers (with or without certification). As Glasbergen (2018: 244–245) emphasized, one needs to look at VSS as an incentive for reform in the political economy of the production of agricultural commodities and food. One should therefore not start research with the problem definition of certification and with how to optimize the certification process (which is the basis of most literature on VSS), but with the real problems smallholder farmers, cooperatives and SMEs are faced with.

VSS may be guided by the public objective of 'more sustainability', but implemented at company-level in a very limited form. Many socially important issues such as poverty reduction, respecting human rights, achieving good governance, specifically contributing to climate change mitigation, and contributing to higher sufficiency in consumption are usually missing in the VSS dialogue.

Many VSS encourage producers to implement measures that improve qualities or product characteristics that are of particular economic and commercial interest of the leading players in the supply chains (e.g. product differentiation, product quality, food safety, an increase of supply base and security of supply). Macro-economic and global sustainability objectives are not or only in a subdue way on the VSS agenda. It is therefore important that any public support to VSS setting and implementation must be linked to the achievement of public environmental and social interests and not private commercial agendas.[43]

VSS are couched within the market-economics logic fostering more production, trade and consumption. In other words, even though some environmental and social VSS requirements dampen undesirable impact of food products and production, generally VSS are part of the growth paradigm. Yet, true sustainability remains elusive without paying due attention to and incorporating aspects of

---

43 Also see Joint Conference Church and Development (2015: 44).
   The ISEAL Alliance developed a number of Credibility Principles for VSS, which are however very broad to be a defining feature here. These principles include: sustainability; improvement; relevance; rigour; engagement; impartiality; transparency; accessibility; truthfulness; and efficiency. For more information, see: www.isealalliance.org/credible-sustainability-standards/iseal-credibility-principles

consumption reduction and sufficiency (for more detail, see Buntzel and Mari, 2016: chapter 9).

E. The Limitations and Cons of VSS

1. Transparency, Openness and Conflict of Interests

A serious challenge, in particular of B2B VSS, remains the assurance of transparency and openness in standard development, but also in the revision of the standards and in defining conformity assessment rules.

According to an OECD study (Gruère, 2013: 29), although transparency and openness in VSS setting has generally increased, still about two-thirds of the reviewed VSS have an opaque standard-setting process.

Another key challenge of VSS setting is the scientific justifiability of standard claims. Are standards addressing real and societally-important risks or are they exclusively or partly driven by perceived risks? While the WTO SPS Agreement (Article 2.2.) insists that SPS measures (that might also be enshrined in standards on food safety) shall be based on scientific principles and not maintained without sufficient scientific evidence (usually based on a recognized needs test), the WTO TBT Agreement (Article 2.2.), which is the more general accord on standards, allows the use of technical regulation and standards when considered necessary to fulfil a 'legitimate objective'.[44] That wording in the TBT Agreement allows a wide scope of VSS measures.[45] This is why some analysts describe the motives for VSS as an 'amalgam of real and perceived risks' (also see Rundgren, 2015). By way of illustration, according to the OECD study (Gruère, 2013: 30), the frequency of the use of life-cycle assessment (LCA) (as attempt of scientific

---

44 As regards the term 'legitimacy', the TBT Agreement is not very specific. It only provides an illustrative list of legitimate objectives, inter alia: national security requirements; the prevention of deceptive practices; protection of human health or safety, animal or plant life or health, or the environment.

45 For instance, the WTO Dispute Panel Report on the US – Tuna II case (initiated by Mexico) states in para. 7.437: 'In this respect, a measure that aims at the protection of animal life or health need not, in our view, be directed exclusively to endangered or depleted species or populations, to be legitimate. Article 2.2 refers to 'animal life or health' in general terms, and does not require that such protection be tied to a broader conservation objective. We therefore read these terms as allowing Members to pursue policies that aim at also protecting individual animals or species whose sustainability as a group is not threatened.'

justification) in the VSS setting process is low.[46] LCA has been used in less than one fifth of the reviewed VSS.

Another issue of concern is the conflict of interests in many VSS schemes, including those developed by NGOs. On the one hand, standard-setting bodies have financial interest in increasing numbers of certified producers; on the other hand, certification auditors are often paid by the producers they are assessing. According to the Changing Markets Foundation (2018: 51, 56, 57), both factors manifest in lenient interpretations of the standards.

The same study also highlights another paradox that applies to several VSS it reviews in the fisheries and textile sectors:

> A perceived imperative to make certification schemes inclusive, rather than selective, has become a major hindrance to driving greater ambition. When schemes and standards are created on the basis of consensus among a wide range of industry players rather than by a vanguard of top performers, there is an inherent danger that the parties will agree to keep the bar low to ensure everyone makes the grade – usually just slightly above the lowest common denominator. (Changing Markets Foundation, 2018: 85)

As a result, many such VSS schemes lack an incentive of continuous improvement.

2. VSS as International Standards and the Problem of Sufficient Local Flexibility

Standards are a key instrument to increase and facilitate communication and exchange of goods and services within a country and across national borders. With increasing internationalization of trade, communication and transport it appears opportune to develop and agree on international standards. According to the WTO Agreements on TBT and SPS measures relevant requirements for traded goods should observe four key principles: non-discrimination; avoidance of unnecessary barriers to trade; transparency; and the use of international standards. For agri-food products, the WTO Agreement on Sanitary and Phytosanitary Measures designated three organizations (in WTO parlance

---

46 While LCA has some merits, it also has a lot of limitations for food and agricultural application. There is the risk of biased approaches and conclusions as a function of (i) selection of criteria; (ii) forming criteria groups or clusters; (iv) giving relative weights to the cluster results for the overall rating; and (v) method of aggregation of cluster results. For a review in this regard, see Rundgren (2020).

also known as the three sisters) as international standard-setting bodies: Codex Alimentarius Commission, the World Organization for Animal Health and the International Plant Protection Convention. Conversely, the TBT Agreement does not designate or refer to any international standard setting body for standards, covering non-food safety related issues. It however recommends the use of 'relevant international standards'.

Therefore, there is ample policy space for countries on the relevance, level and appropriateness of standards. Instead of a specific definition of 'international standard' in the TBT Agreement, the TBT Committee (in Annex 4 of the Second Triennial Review of the TBT Agreement) agreed upon a list of procedural requirements to develop such standards, which includes the following six principles: transparency; openness; impartiality and consensus; relevance and effectiveness; coherence; and the development dimension (TBT Committee decision G/TBT/9, 13 November 2000).[47]

As a result, outside the scope of international standards set by the abovementioned 'three sisters', any organization, group or company can set a standard and declare it of international character, provided the standard has a sufficient international commercial weight and recognition, and generally observes the six recommended (procedural) principles by the TBT Committee.

In practice, however, it is rather challenging to observe in particular the principles of relevance and effectiveness, coherence, and the development dimension. The lion's share of such VSS with an international scope tend to set the requirements, control points and testing protocols according to the situation and interests in developed countries. Such standards then pretend that the relevant requirements are of global relevance. This ignores at least three cases of required diversity: (i) nature, weather and climate differ around the globe and have a significant bearing on agricultural production conditions and related risks; (ii) there are cultural and social differences in appreciating norms and behaviour; and (iii) diversity in production patterns and conditions plays a significant role in and for agriculture. It is therefore important that international VSS provide for a sufficient flexibility in either accommodating these divergent conditions or allow for forms of standard implementation that interpret the requirements, related control points and testing protocols in a flexible way. It might be worth adding that it

---

47 Annex 4 of the document is entitled Decision of the Committee on Principles for the Development of International Standards, Guides and Recommendations with relation to Articles 2, 5, and Annex 3 of the Agreement. Available at: www.docsonline.wto.org

is difficult to communicate to consumers that the actual implementation of the standards are different. In the case of commodities, which are also produced in the importing country, this is even more difficult as domestic producers in the importing country may lobby against the fact that imports are not subject to the same rules as they have to follow – all very visible in the organic sector.

By way of illustration, IFOAM[48] has traditionally pursued a strategy of developing IFOAM Basic Standards (a sort of framework), on the basis of which national organic standards (no matter whether mandatory or voluntary) could be developed, reflecting national specificities. Conceptually, the GlobalGAP standard also provided for some flexibility through so-called national interpretative guidelines, which could be developed by a national working group in preparation of a national GAP (Good Agricultural Practice) standard (for example KenyaGAP, ChinaGAP or ThaiGAP). Yet, with the benefit of hindsight, evidence suggests that the lion's share of GAP-compliant fresh food exports from developing to developed countries were certified under the original GlobalGAP and not the commercial, nationally developed GAP standards.

In short, the emphasis on the use of relevant international standards imposes conditions and requirements underlying VSS on all producers, no matter how diverse their production conditions are. Stipulations for instance on agro-chemical use, crop sequence, soil and plant protection management are fixed unrelated to divergent national circumstances and thus appear like externally imposed. This unilateral dependence and hegemony undermines the capability of local farmers in developing countries to deal with and manage local agricultural conditions creatively.

What is required therefore is a careful trade-off between the pros of international VSS for international trade and the avoidance of unnecessary discrimination, on the one hand, and the imperative of national and local flexibility in responding to different environmental and social conditions, their bearing on production conditions and creative responses to deal with them. Otherwise, such VSS are seen as cementing domination and unilateral dependence.

---

48 The International Federation of Organic Agriculture Movements (IFOAM – Organics International), founded in 1972, is the worldwide umbrella organization for the organic agriculture movement, which represents close to 800 affiliates in 117 countries. Its mission is to lead, unite and assist the organic movement in its full diversity, as well as the worldwide adoption of ecologically, socially and economically sound systems, based on the Principles of Organic Agriculture. For more information, see: www.ifoam.bio

Besides, there is also the risk that such international VSS contain requirements and stipulate management approaches that are based on existing external-input-intensive and factory-farming like agricultural production in the North (for example through obligations on agro-chemical management or product tracing). This implies that farmers in developing countries find themselves locked into agro-technological approaches that are investment-intensive, and from which it is difficult, if not impossible to withdraw. The economic stability of farmers is being endangered by external-input and fixed-capital-intensive production, because this fuels indebtedness. Except for standards on organic agriculture, most VSS lack incentives and leverage on transiting to agro-ecological or agro-forestry production methods and extensive livestock raring that are all more labour and knowledge-intensive and better suited to smallholder farmers in developing countries.

3. Inclusion or Exclusion: Can VSS Really Work for Smallholder Farmers?

The market mechanism encourages shifts and outsourcing of production to least-costly locations (i.e. absolute competitive advantage), but also leads to shifts in competitive position to producers that comply with VSS in the least-costly way. This causes cost pressure, encourages specialization and increasing scale of production and underpins the marginalization of small-scale producers and smallholder farmers, all things that often undermine or contradict truly sustainable production. The whole architecture of VSS is very challenging for small-scale farmers.

To put this issue into the socio-economic development process in developing countries and to avoid the impression that rural employment and rural communities are losing importance, suffice it to bear in mind that even in China and India – the two most populous rapidly industrializing countries – between 43 and 60 percent of the workforce is still engaged in agriculture, over 640 million people in all. Even in countries such as Thailand, Turkey and Morocco, 40–50 percent of the national workforce is involved in agriculture. In LDCs this figure often reaches 70–80 percent, if indirect or part-time activities in agriculture are included.[49]

---

49 WTO document WT/GC/W/765/Rev.2 (4 March 2019). The Continued Relevance of Special and Differential Treatment in Favour of Developing Members to Promote Development and Ensure Inclusiveness. Para 2.10. Also see: Vorley and Proctor (2008).

As will be elaborated on below, it cannot be overemphasized that achieving economic sustainability in implementing VSS is key for smallholders as social and ecological sustainability become illusive without a solid economic foundation.

The production methods that are required by smallholder farmers under VSS schemes generally completely differ from their traditional farming methods. Traditional farming knowledge is invalidated – site or location-specific practices for soil-quality preservation, crop rotation and combination, polyculture, integrated farming, closed nutrient cycles and biodiversity preservation, to name but the most important. Many VSS schemes rather require specialization, economies of scale and external-input intensive mono-cropping. Such strategies always tend to result in 'selective development paths', because only few smallholder farmers, who can turn themselves into entrepreneurs and manage to obtain technical, training and financial support from public and private sources, actually manage to stay in VSS schemes under international supply chains (see also Buntzel, 2020: 134–135).

In reality, however, smallholder farmers can hardly afford the required investment for adapting production facilities to VSS and bearing the additional costs for standard implementation and certification. Many smallholders are also illiterate and the documentation and recording requirements of most agri-food VSS therefore represent an almost insurmountable hurdle, which may only be cleared in the context of well-organized producer groups. Smallholders can only stay in VSS systems if increased fixed capital and implementation-related costs are evened out by increases in productivity or by higher quality premiums, which, as will be shown later, is the exception rather than the rule. As a result, unless public or private donors provide considerable financial support or subsidies to smallholders almost on a permanent basis, just like blood transfusion, it is unlikely that many smallholders can become and remain part of VSS systems for a number of years.

Bill Vorley, the coordinator of the IIED project on Regoverning Markets: Small-scale Producers in Modern Agrifood Markets (Vorley, 2013: 29), drawing on 36 case studies in 17 countries concludes that

> only a small subset of producers – perhaps 2 to 10 per cent – can easily step up to commercial sales in modern value chains. Bringing a larger pool of smaller-scale and poorer farmers into the game requires a rare combination of institutions: effective producers' organisations, receptive buyers, a facilitating policy and effective brokering. Without such an arrangement, efforts to link smallholders to modern markets can remain stuck in the pilot stage and dependent on project funds.

Certification of producer groups to facilitated smallholder involvement in VSS schemes is an option contained in several VSS (of the 181 VSS included in the ITC Standards Map data base in 2016, 76 VSS offered group certification) (ITC/EUI, 2016: 16). Producer groups significantly vary in their type, structure and size.[50] Group certification can undoubtedly drive group formation and the professionalization of existing producer groups, provided that these groups are well organized and managed. However, according to a study of Aidenvironment it appears that many strong producer groups, supply chain-based and service provider groups operate mainly on donor funding if it concerns certification. This shows that no matter which model is used, subsidies are often a precondition, or at least an important driver, to invest in certification of small-scale producers (Molenaar et al., 2011).

Buntzel and Mari (2016: chapter 21) correctly underline the fact that the principal question for the development relevance of smallholder agriculture is not whether one succeeds in incorporating one or the other farmer or producer in the group of 'selected or dedicated producers' in supply chains, but how generally relevant the model of standards, contract farming, value chains and agricultural exports is. Does it have the potential to effectively combat rural poverty and encourage and facilitate the transformation to truly sustainable agriculture? Is the model confined to some more well-placed and developed enclaves or can it also penetrate marginal areas? This naturally raises the strategic question of whether one wants that 10–20 percent of farmers improve their sustainability parameters by 80–90 percent or whether 80–90 percent of farmers lift their sustainability record by 10–20 percent.

VSS are an element in a wider set of a Western-style 'modernization of food systems'. It necessarily goes along with other elements, like contract farming, seed regulations, land registration, value chain management, and the supermarket model.[51] This mode of food production and distribution must have an alternative for poor societies. What such alternative could look like is still an open question.

---

50 The main types of producer groups are: (i) producer-based groups: cooperatives and producer associations; informal and registered producer groups; communal land groups; (ii) supply chain-based groups: contract farming or outgrower schemes; trader networks; sharecropping and tenant farming arrangements; business ventures with mixed ownership; and (iii) service provider networks: public, private or non-profit driven.

51 It should not go without comment that the habits and rationality of poor people in many developing countries do not comply with the 'Western Style' *homo economicus* and especially the fact that many of the VSS prescriptions are ethnocentric.

Achieving economic sustainability of VSS-compliant smallholders is of paramount importance for avoiding their drop out from certification schemes. Real cost internalization through fair and cooperative marketing systems can potentially play a critical role in this regard. However, in many cases smallholders are made part of contract farming systems that lock farmers in select input purchase and product sales' systems that create relations of unilateral dependence, market domination and border, at least in some cases, on forms of modern slavery (for a more elaborate review, see Oxfam, 2018: 38).

Often it is argued that if smallholders become VSS-compliant they can benefit from quality premiums and from higher productivity through upgrading production methods and organization of production. Having extensively studied the situation of cocoa producers in Nicaragua and vegetable farmers in Kenya, Krauss and Krishnan of the University of Manchester concluded that this assumption is often flawed.[52] While certification may allow Northern companies to access premium price segments, for producers the costs of sustainability standards often outweigh economic benefits. The authors highlight that the power and embeddedness dynamics governing global value chains will have a considerable impact on whose power will lead to the projection of whose priorities will prevail, confirming the primacy of corporate power and private-sector stakeholders' commercial interests over producers' priorities. The results of their research equally underline that process and product upgrading activities, which may allow Northern buyers to access premium markets, may not necessarily entail an improved economic, social or environmental situation for Southern producers. Similarly, despite the improved capacity-building and organizational opportunities, which certification schemes may entail, improved bargaining power is by no means an automatism, requiring careful unpacking (Krauss and Krishnan, 2016: 28–29).

---

52 Research by the TransSustain group at the University of Muenster in Germany on the improvement of livelihoods of Colombian coffee cooperatives through VSS use comes to similar conclusions: 'We found that the addition of private and industry-led certifications makes minimal difference to smallholders' economy, and thus do not offer a viable path out of poverty for coffee farmers' (TransSustain, 2020).

Even if there were willingness of developing country governments to provide flanking support, the extent and the costs of it would be extremely high and demanding. The legal, technical and infrastructural capacity-building needs for effective VSS implementation are generally so immense that the budgetary burdens might eat up most of the public agricultural investments. For developed countries this a far less onerous problem, and that is part of the unfair competition VSS create in global trade.[53]

One has to consider priorities for developing countries as well. They often lack resources to uphold basic, regulatory hygiene, environment, social and safety standards, and it is difficult to justify that they should allocate many resources to implement schemes that go much further than the regulatory requirements at a time when they are not yet met. That holds both for the governments' own activities and support to producers, advisory services etc. Yet, this crowding-out effect of VSS has been very evident in several developing countries in recent years.[54]

With the exception of few developing countries, in many others there is a serious lack of the most basic personnel, infrastructural and technical capacity for effective food quality and safety control. This includes efficient and trustworthy institutions, well-equipped testing laboratories accredited according to ISO-Guidelines, inspectors, scientific research bodies and certifying bodies, to name but the most important.[55] This means that most of the related services will

---

53 According to the already quoted WTO document WT/GC/W/765/Rev.2, paragraph 2.9.: 'In 2016, the domestic support per farmer in the United States was $60,586; the corresponding figures for some other WTO Members were the following: Japan ($10,149), Canada ($16,562), the European Union ($6,762), China ($863), Brazil ($345) and India ($227). Thus, the per farmer subsidy in the United States was 70 times that in China, 176 times that in Brazil and 267 times that in India. Per farmer subsidy in Japan was 12 times that in China, 29 times that in Brazil and 45 times that in India. Per farmer subsidy in Canada was 19 times that in China, 48 times that in Brazil and 73 times that in India. In the European Union, per farmer subsidy was 8 times that in China, 20 times that in Brazil and 30 times that in India.'

54 In Kenya, for instance, in the early 2000s informal discussions took place within the Horticultural Crops Development Agency (HCDA) of the Ministry of Agriculture and the Fresh Produce Exporters Association of Kenya (FPEAK) whether the nationally developed commercial KenyaGAP standard should eventually be converted into a national (public) GAP standard. In some other developing countries, modular systems later emerged that were based on public national quality assurance systems (such as the Q-GAP system in Thailand), but supplemented by private commercial GAP standards (like ThaiGAP) to facilitate exports, as these were benchmarked to the GlobalGAP standard. For more information in this regard, see: Hoffmann and Vossenaar (2007).

55 Some rare exceptions in this regard are, for instance, the Quality Council of India (part of the Department for Promotion of Industry and International Trade) and The National Institute

have to be acquired from abroad, and this is bound to reduce the benefits for the exporting country.

Governmental investment in and support for technical, organizational and communication infra-structure as well as research and training would be imperative. Yet, in particular in Africa, the structural adjustment programs of the World Bank and the IMF in the 1980s and 1990s led to the discontinuation of such public efforts and significantly reduced the constructive governmental role (for example, most national commodity boards, which were also in charge of quality grading and quality assurance, had to be abolished). Also, the implementation of the Maputo Declaration, i.e. the Declaration on Agriculture and Food Security in Africa that was adopted by the Heads of State and Government of the African Union (AU) in July 2003, calling upon AU member countries to spend no less than 10 percent of national government budgets on agriculture within 5 years, had rather disappointing results.[56]

While VSS mostly apply to sales for international value chains, the lion's share of small-scale producers and farmers generate their income on local markets. An excessive export-orientation and the support by the donor community of the integration of smallholders in global supply chains may therefore underutilize the potential of local markets for pro-poor development, food security and food sovereignty as well as rural livelihoods.[57]

In most developing countries, including China and more so in India, there exists a competitive sector of small and medium-scale retail businesses, most of it being part of the informal sector.[58] Can they cautiously be 'modernized' outside the conventional Western supermarket model? What would be standards and

of Metrology, Standardization and Industrial Quality (INMETRO) in Brazil, which is linked to the Ministry of Development, Industry and Foreign Trade. Both are examples of government institutions that coordinate standard-related policies and technical issues in a cross-departmental way.

56 In the period till 2015, only 11 African countries managed to allocate 10 percent or more of their public budgets to agriculture in any year since 2005 (Fontan Sers and Mughal, 2018: 3).

57 In many cases, despite the middle-men and all other issues with the informal sector, small-holders might be better off servicing that sector than international value chains. For a more elaborate analysis, see: www.iied.org/harnessing-potential-zambias-informal-food-sector and https://includeplatform.net/wp-content/uploads/2019/07/one-pager-informal-sector-INCLUDE.pdf

58 Even in one of the best organized cities in India, Bangalore, it is estimated that only about one fifth of all food is sold in the organized (formal) food market. Some 50 million smallholder farmers in China supply through about 5 million middlemen many of the big mega-cities in the eastern part of the country with food without being integrated in value chains, outgrower

a standard-setting procedure that is inclusive for smallholder farmers and poor consumers, and at the same time respectful to social and environmental issues?

Against this background, there is far too much attention devoted in research and policy discussions to VSS and international supply chains. This distracts attention from the role of national markets, informal trade and retail as well as the most pressing needs for improving national food safety and reducing related ecological, environmental and social risks.

There is a lot of debate in certain developing countries, such as in India, Kenya, Viet Nam or Thailand, whether they should introduce next to the global VSS also a simpler national standard, which is more appropriate for the domestic conditions. That this debate takes place is a 'spillover' from the dominance and operation of global VSS in their food export sectors and the insight that those may be inappropriate for the smallholders and petit traders that prevail at home. Many countries have established National Standard Authorities, but they mostly restrict their role to mandatory hygienic standards. The majority of experts are of the opinion that the co-existence of two or several different food standards side by side may not work easily and without conflict in the long run, because of the increasing role of domestic supermarkets, the involvement of foreign corporations and the competition with certified imports on their food systems.[59]

---

systems or vertical integration through supermarkets. Despite Kenya's GAP export initiatives, no less than 80 percent of produced fruit and vegetables are domestically sold through informal markets. See: Buntzel and Mari (2016: chapter 22).

59 An UNCTAD study (Hoffmann and Vossenaar, 2007: 28–29) on GAP schemes in several ASEAN countries made the following recommendations in this regard: There should be a 'gradual approach to GAP implementation: ASEAN countries should continue to gradually upgrade their national GAP schemes, taking into account domestic needs as well as international buyers' requirements. A top priority of GAP implementation in ASEAN countries should be to help prepare farmers to meet food safety requirements (in particular pesticide use and Maximum Residue Levels - MRLs), and to provide them with incentives to comply with national food safety regulations. Emphasis on the appropriate registration and use of plant protection products also helps in protecting the occupational health and safety of rural workers. GAP schemes can gradually include other objectives, including environmental management and workers' welfare issues. A two-tier approach could promote a scheme consisting of a "basic" standard for local requirements and an "export" standard to meet the requirements of private sector standards in premium markets such as the EU. Farmers could then satisfy the immediate requirements of the domestic market while moving gradually towards meeting the more demanding "export" standards. As the case of Thailand illustrates, modular approaches to GAP schemes are emerging. In Thailand's case, this consists of a national, government-run GAP scheme, directly GlobalGAP-certified companies, regional GAP schemes benchmarked to GlobalGAP and a ThaiGAP . . . benchmarked to GlobalGAP. Such approach however calls

F. Can VSS-Governed Sustainability Markets Really be Mainstreamed and Graduate from Current Market Niches?

Mainstreaming of VSS-compliant production is often simplistically perceived as a linear process. Quite a number of VSS protagonists believe that public procurement linked to VSS[60] and VSS-compliant sales' targets set by large companies would be the key drivers.[61]

As market shares however increase, competition from other VSS-compliant, but also non-certified producers intensifies, which leads to a so-called cost-treadmill effect (see Box 5).

Box 5: Understanding the 'Cost Treadmill Trap' and its implications for VSS-compliant producers

To start with, it should not be overlooked that many VSS schemes are B2B models that are not at all associated with price premiums for producers. They are 'producer-pay-to-play' schemes.[62]

As market shares of VSS-compliant sales rise and the number of VSS increases, producers are faced with intensified (cost) competition from other VSS-compliant producers, and non-certified production (part of it also moving its production characteristics closer to VSS requirements).

As a result, price premiums for VSS-compliant products, if not entirely or mostly appropriated by supermarkets or food processors, shrink or disappear altogether. There are also severe asymmetries in value-added appropriation along the

---

for a coherent design of the modules aimed at: (i) assuring the integrity of the whole system, (ii) allowing graduation from simpler to more advanced modules, and (iii) the creation of interfaces between the modules. All this should serve to avoid confusion among producers and consumers, ease access to domestic and foreign markets and reduce or optimize certification costs.'

60 The revised WTO plurilateral Agreement on Government Procurement of 2011 includes a work programme on the treatment of sustainable procurement.

61 Even some NGOs and international organizations surprisingly seem to share such views. By way of illustration: ITC (2016) or ITC, IISD, FiBL (2019).

62 The term was coined in discussions with Bill Vorley, based on his experience as project coordinator of the IIED project on Regoverning Markets: Small-scale Producers in Modern Agrifood Markets.

supply chain because of power imbalance (producer's share in retail price has continuously dropped).[63]

Furthermore, because of stiff competition a rather significant share of VSS-compliant production cannot be sold as certified, but has to be unloaded in the non-certified (conventional) market at its prevailing prices.[64] To make matters worse, a not insignificant volume of VSS-compliant production, which is turned down by international purchasers for reasons of real or ostensible insufficient quality or at times of oversupply, also tends to end up in national and international markets for non-certified produce, thus exacerbating cost and price pressure.[65]

Higher income from productivity and quality improvements does often not even out additional costs for investment in adjusting production to comply with VSS requirements as well as for inspection and certification costs. Higher productivity also tends to increase the risk of supply-demand imbalances in international agro-food markets and may thus result in depressed or volatile prices.[66]

Product innovation to counter the treadmill effect often takes place further downstream in the value chain.

The implications of all points flagged above are:

- There is a trend of market concentration towards well organized and larger producers and the resulting marginalization of smallholders.

63 When one buys a cup of coffee for say 2 Euro, the farmer gets 3–4 cents for the coffee in that cup. If one buys a cup of VSS-certified coffee (such as Rainforest Alliance, 4C, UTZ, organic or Fairtrade) one may have to cough-up 2.50 Euro and the farmer will get 4–5 cents. The farmer's income will increase by an impressive 20–25 percent. Looking at it from another perspective though, it seems that one needs to spend 50 cents to increase the farmer's income by 1 or 2 cents. This example throws up the question whether the market mechanism is efficient in transforming consumers' willingness to pay for direct or indirect benefits of a product (Rundgren, 2017).

64 In 2016, of all coffee grown and certified as Fairtrade, for instance, only a third was sold at the Fairtrade minimum price; two thirds were 'dumped' in the conventional market. For cocoa, the rate was a bit better at 47 percent, whereas it was much worse for tea at only 4.7 percent (Subramanian, 2019). Comparing the volume of standard-compliant production with standard-certified sales for the year 2012 for a number of agro-food products across all applied VSS, Potts et al. (2014: 91) find that with the exception of bananas and cotton VSS-certified sales only account for between one quarter and half of VSS-compliant production volume.

65 Therefore, the market of VSS-compliant produce and the domestic market for conventional food products have no neutral relationship – the former instrumentalizes and abuses the latter for its purposes.

66 Such effects are apparent on a macro level. Nevertheless and regardless of certification, from the perspective of individual producers or a producer group higher productivity is still interesting in most cases.

- There is a switch towards less demanding and usually also less costly VSS (in coffee, for instance, from organic, Fairtrade and Rainforest Alliance to 4C).[67]
- The risk of fraud is increasing.[68]
- There is also increasing likelihood that certification is not renewed or farmers formally exit from VSS schemes.

This is reinforced by the power imbalance between producers and large buyers along the supply chain. Thus, any internalization of externalities becomes difficult and the economic sustainability of VSS-compliant producers is put in jeopardy. This is the most challenging dilemma for many VSS-compliant producers (except large-scale and well-resourced once), to which there are as yet no or only imperfect remedies. The cost-treadmill effect applies to producers both in developing and developed countries.

Evidence from market-share expansion expectations for organic and Fairtrade products, for instance, suggests that increasing market shares has been slower and more problem-laden than expected. Commercial interest in market expansion increasingly collides with safeguarding the integrity and principles of organic and Fairtrade products. The pressure exerted by large, including institutional investors in expanding production and market shares may coerce farmers to fall victim to the traps of conventional, industrial agriculture: economies of scale, specialization, driving up labour productivity at the expense of resource mining, and pressure to dilute standards and/or their enforcement. This jeopardizes smallholder

---

67 According to the TransSustain Program at the University of Muenster in Germany, about 60 percent of sustainable coffee available on the market is certified by sustainability standards at the lower end of the demanding standards, while only approximately 34 percent of the total volume of certified coffee adheres to standards on the higher end. This indicates that there is a relative race to the bottom occurring in the sector as VSS-certified coffee becomes mainstream (TransSustain Policy Brief, 2019).

The Voluntary Coffee Standards Index (VOCSI), developed by the TransSustain Programme, ranks existing sustainability standards from 1 to 14, with certifications that designate a focus on smallholders broken out separately, based on results in four categories: Environmental, Social, Economic and Enforcement. Researchers analysed the institutional design of each standard, then identified 92 distinct regulatory topics to weigh them against initially assigning points from 0 to 3 in each of the four main categories. In addition, the group conducted interviews with 17 coffee sustainability experts, who awarded additional points.

68 See for instance for the case of tea Sennholz-Weinhardt (2019).

farmers, agro-ecological and agro-forestry farming as well as the assurance of economic sustainability and living incomes.

G. 'Organic' – A Standard with a Different Touch

1. Evolution of 'Organic'

The 'mother' of all standards in the sphere of food and agriculture is the one on 'organic' (synonymous with 'BIO'). One specific version of it, called 'bio-dynamic', since 1928 marketed through the label 'Demeter', is the oldest VSS connected to food and agriculture. It goes back to the lectures by the Austrian philosopher Rudolf Steiner from Mai 1924. Since the 1970s other versions of the same basic idea of how to perform agriculture in a pure organic way emerged in many countries. For instance, the 'Bioland' standard was founded in Germany in 1974. Today there are more than 12 different private 'organic' standard organizations in Germany alone; they operate their own organic labels with slightly different versions of 'organic', and they all provide connected services. The organic standard – also a voluntary sustainability standard – differs considerably from the 'other VSS' in many respects, even if there is a tendency of convergence by economic pressure and inherent contradictions.[69]

The idea of organic agriculture spread around the globe after the Second World War, leading to the formation of the global umbrella organization IFOAM (International Federation of Organic Agricultural Movements) in 1972. This was the first attempt to turn a conceptual idea into a defined set of global minimum criteria for 'organic', and the establishment of a Third Party Audit procedure. Nowadays IFOAM has 819 affiliated member organizations on all continents, 135 of them are supporting organizations, many of the others are farmers' organizations.

IFOAM developed and adopted the Principles of Organic Agriculture in 2005, defining a global benchmark for the common understanding on what organic agriculture is about.[70] No other standard in food and agriculture is based

---

69 For clarity of language and terminology: we talk about 'organic' as the private VSS, 'organic public regulated' as the legally defined (mandatory) standard, and on 'other VSS' as the commercial standards on conventional agriculture and food products.

70 The Four Principles are: 'Health' (of soil, plant, animal and humans), 'Ecology' (living ecological systems and cycles), 'Fairness' (relationship that ensures fairness) and 'Care' (precautionary and responsible manner for the future and the environment).

on such formalized ethical framework.[71] The Principles do not lead directly to a technical standard, but rather to guidelines that leave enough flexibility for each affiliated country/regional association to define their own specific regionally adapted version of organic. IFOAM does not operate a standard or label, but acts more like a mediator, advocacy organization, coordinator of certification procedures, research and counsellor to its members, serving the objective to spread the idea of organic agriculture around the world. Organic standards do not follow a formalized framework of ethical principles, they stick to a set of instructions. Other VSS never question the agro-food system, but rather aim for incremental improvement and gains. Therefore, they do not address systemic, structural and core socio-economic issues.

2. What Makes 'Organic' Special?

In comparison to 'organic', other VSS emerged somewhat later. The forces that made them evolve were quite different from the evolution of 'organic': not the farmers, who were dissatisfied with the prevailing agronomic model, were the initiators of the other VSS, but business – especially traders, who wanted to manage liability and risks, and exploit green consumerism as emerging trend. GlobalGAP, for instance, emerged on the pillars of EurepGAP (Euro-Retailer Produce Working Group), which started in 1997 through the cooperation of 17 supermarket chains in Europe; UTZ-Kapeh ('Good Coffee' in the Mayan language Quiché), which was launched in 2002 by a coffee grower (Nick Bocklandt, a Belgian-Guatemalan coffee farmer) and Ward de Groote, a Dutch coffee roaster, with the goal of implementing sustainability on a large scale in the worldwide market.; Rainforest Alliance goes back to 1986, an establishment by one person, a US environmentalist; the 4C-Association (Common Code of the Coffee Community) was an initiative of the German Technical Cooperation Agency (GTZ), a publically funded technical assistance agency, launched in 2006.

The basic functioning of 'other VSS' and 'organic' looks quite similar. Both follow a self-assigned agronomic technical standard, which promises a conversion of real business into products and management systems claiming to serve some higher societal goals (like sustainability, ecology, social diligence, fairness). Both certify producers and their products with a label at a premium price or without

---

71 See Freyer and Bingen (2014: 281–313). An exception is the 'agroecology' movement, which very much resembles that of the original 'organic', however without running a labelling program (see Migliorini and Wezel, 2017: 37–63).

a label, simply to take the opportunity to access discerning markets. Both run a system to preserve the integrity of their products. Many of the auditors around the world, who verify standards, certify producers of 'organic' and under 'other VSS'. Certifiers need to be accredited by national (public or private) accreditation bodies.

While 'other VSS' follow their own defined criteria of sustainability, and stand in for 'Good Agricultural Practices – GAP' on environmental, managerial, some social and economic indicators, organic standards adhere to the global principles of IFOAM. 'Organic' claims to work for a holistic transformation of agricultural systems and supply chains and implies to be a fair, safe and caring alternative to the industrial model in food and agriculture. The objective of organic standards is a food economy, which abstains from agrochemicals, food alteration and genetic modification, serves the farmers to make a living on their land, maintains biodiversity and natural resources and takes into account that regional conditions require locally adapted solutions, incorporating the traditional knowledge of the farming community. Up to a certain point the organic movement challenges abstract capitalist relations that fuel exploitation in the global agro-food system. Recently the organic movement also claims that their methods of farming are more climate-friendly, although some of their global supply chains do not necessarily follow that line, causing as much 'food mileage' as conventional products.[72]

3. Basic Differences between 'Organic' and 'Other VSS'

One of the major differences between other VSS and organic standards came about when the organic movement successfully lobbied for governmental recognition and international equivalence on the definition of 'organic' by EU-Regulation 2092/91 (Regulation 834/2007 replaced the 2092/91 in 2007), using the existing IFOAM definitions as a template, trying to protect consumers from fraudulent use of the terms 'bio', 'organic' and 'environmental'.[73] However the EU-Regulation is confined to the agronomic side of 'organic', the social, cultural

---

72 It should not go without comment that most organic movements emphasize the importance of local and regional marketing as well as the development of commensurate local and regional marketing networks, inter alia to strengthen or implement various forms of community-supported agriculture.

73 EC Regulation 834/2007 and 889/2008 (https://ec.europa.eu/info/food-farming-fisheries/ farming/ organic-farming/legislation_en).

and fairness parts of the IFOAM principles are not included. This implied a 'friendly takeover' of the marketing standard of 'organic' by the state. As of 2018, 91 countries have similar legislation, another 16 countries are in the drafting process, and 29 countries have a national or regional organic standard (FiBL/ IFOAM, 2019: 52 ff.). The governmental actions are based on the Guidelines for an international standard for 'organic', developed by the Codex Alimentarius Commission (1999/2001), which is recognized by the WTO as one of the three competent international standard setting organizations in the field of food and agriculture.

The state regulations are only basic, just setting a ground floor for 'organic', leaving space for the many IFOAM member organizations to continue to run their own private labels and certification programs. These private organic labels must also adhere to the public organic standard, but complement it by their own, more ambitious criteria with respect to specific local solutions and concerns, like in matters of seed breeding, bio-pesticides or animal welfare. This kind of hybrid or dual-track approach for a standard program is unique. It provides to the organic standard credentials and legal protection against green washing and ideological attacks.[74] However, at the same time it makes the movement also vulnerable to governmental intervention.[75] It implies that for organic food production there is a surveillance system based on double checks: by the public authority and a control body of the private label. In comparison to the 'other VSS', organic farmers have to bear more serious consequences of misconduct, because violation of the state organic standard (legally a regulation) can be considered as a criminal offence.

No objective claimed by any other VSS has received this kind of public respect.[76] There is no clear understanding or even protected definition of what

74 At a point in the 1970s, the Swiss Government was about to ban all claims on 'bio' and 'organic'. Conventional Farmers Unions tried to discredit organic agriculture by claiming that conventional agriculture was also 'biological', because even agrochemicals were based on natural laws.

75 The US Department of Agriculture (USDDA), for instance, had allowed under the National Organic Program (NOP) to certify hydroponic production as 'organic' against the fierce opposition by many stakeholders from the organic movement. In the EU, the conflicting governance by the State and the organic movement became evident over the plans of the EU Commission to revise the Organic Regulation in 2014, heavily disputed by various organic organizations. The EU wanted to include the residue issue into the quality assessment. The same applies to the EU-Commission's proposal on organic seed certification, which would have prompted conventional breeders to take over this market niche.

76 With the exception of the AOs (Appellation of Origins): PGIs (protected geographical indicators), PDO (protected designation of origin) and TSGs (traditional specialties guaranteed), which protect the names of products coming from a specific region and follow a

'sustainability' really stands for. Thus the target is undefined by societal consensus and left to arbitrary interpretation by the commercial VSS. They can shape their reference points according to their utility and commercial interest. As time went by and VSS gained ground in the business world, some of their sustainability criteria became looser. Recently more and more multinational food corporations have started their in-house-developed VSS (but some tendencies in the organic movement are also not immune to an erosion of the original principles, as will be discussed below).

This leads us to the next significant difference: To whom are the standard organizations accountable? Except that all standards are dependent upon public trust, monitored by the media and supervised by their membership, their constituencies differ sharply. The majority of IFOAM's members are farmers' organizations, whose members are congruent with the producers, who carry the major burdens (and benefits) of compliance; the standard-takers are their own standard setters. Organic agriculture originated from local farmers' knowledge and experience.[77] The majority of organic initiatives started with the complete absence of anything like a standard or legal norm. Therefore, the governance structure of the organic movement promotes participation, decentralization and diversity. Even if the labelling and marketing is an integral part of 'organic' today, the soul of the movement goes way beyond the marketing aspect of the label. For many IFOAM members, especially in developing countries, the transformational aspect of 'organic' still is the core, focusing on research, experience sharing, awareness building, soil management and advocacy. The organic activists want to find solutions on how to improve their farming systems in a way to increase the production of the whole farm with holistic methods that simultaneously improve yields and the quality of the soil and guarantee the reproduction of all resources; they act as a learning community.[78]

particular traditional production process/prescription. However, they cannot be called VSS, because they are run by governments, even if they are identified by labels. See: https://ec.europa.eu/info/food-farming-fisheries/food-safety-and-quality/certification/quality-labels/ quality-schemes-explained

77 The first professorship at a European University on organic agriculture was established as late as in the 1980s, a long time after millions of farmers successfully practised organic agriculture.

78 Uganda, for instance, is the country with the highest number of organic farmers in Africa – some 210.000 (FiBL/IFOAM, 2019: 179). But only very few of them are certified and produce for the export market. Their organic movement, NOGAMU, primarily stands for promoting an idea of how to improve farming methods by collective learning with low external input systems.

Even if most of the other VSS might also offer some similar services, they hardly are free of charge, and mainly top down, based on superior expert knowledge. Their objective is not the transformation of the agricultural system, but just to correct some of its shortcomings in order to strengthen conventional markets by offering additional products with a distinctive identity. Always the saleable product is the objective, the managerial feature is just to attach some surplus value associated with market differentiation. In contrast to that, the organic certification does not really certify products, but an alternative production method imbedded within another farming system. The objective is not the labeled product as such, say an organic tomato, but a tomato which originates from an organic farm produced within a diverse farm product portfolio that reflects local specificities in production conditions and follows a reproductive approach to local resources.

4. The Commercial Success Leads to Capitalistic Competition

Both the 'other VSS' and 'organic' have been enormously successful in global markets. As highlighted above, the big standard organizations have certified several million producers globally, and their total share in cropland under certification and their share in markets have been on a steady rise. Despite that, however, it has to be acknowledged that sustainability-standard-compliant production still accounts for just a minor niche in global markets.[79] Worldwide 69,8 million hectares of crops or grassland have come under organic certification programs, encompassing 2.9 million producers in 120 countries, serving the markets by a turn-over of US$92 billion in 2017 (FiBL/IFOAM, 2019: 34 ff.). However, some of the 'other VSS', especially UTZ/RFA, have recently outgrown organic standards in numbers and size.

Partly the lagged growth of 'organic' stems from self-set limitations. The movement never intended to produce expensive food for niche-markets to serve rich people's demand. The goal was to keep accessibility to 'organic' for all consumers and all producers. From the beginning of its economic success, the movement got split between those, who put more emphasis on the ethical and ecological values of the IFOAM Principles, and others, who were more interested in the commercial success.[80] The organic movement is therefore heterogeneous. There

---

79 While the organic movement publishes very detailed statistics every year (sea FiBL/IFOAM), the commercial VSS are not very transparent about the numbers of the cropland covered and sales made.

80 See, for instance, the controversy about BIO 3.0 (Niggli and Plagge, 2015).

is a contradiction within the organic movement between the IFOAM-Principles and the commercial use of a label, if solely for the purpose of processing and marketing organic products. This happens more and more also by corporations, which adhere to the 'harsh' capitalistic market principles. Therefore, 'organic' can well be considered to be at a crossroads (see Sligh and Cierpka, 2007: 30–40 ff.).

The organic movement seems to be the victim of its own success. With the expansion of the organic markets and global trade, the movement partly moved into the direction of agribusiness, and it got subordinated to the dynamics of capitalist markets. This trend makes it more and more difficult for the farming community to maintain equilibrium between the original 'organic ideals' and 'organic as a business'. Companies, which are not committed to the philosophy, gain a foothold in the processing, marketing and even the regulating bodies for labelling/certification of 'organic', which weakens the standards in order to break barriers to entry of business-minded players (large agro-food and trading companies, as well as institutional investors). Also the influence of the State tends to work in the same direction.

Per se, 'organic' is at odds with the marketing by supermarkets. Organic movements suspected that supermarkets' pursuit of profit is largely inconsistent with environmental and ethical concerns. Their insistence on elaborate packaging, uniform produce size and quality, their restrictive business practices and their obsession with economies of scale mean that they are part of a different conceptual approach, which is incompatible with the organic principles (see Tate, 1994: 33).

The integration of the organic movement into the growth of international food markets did not happen without conflict. It took place against strong forces of competition for market access and fair pricing. At the beginning of the successful organic marketing producers could count on remunerative price premiums and secure outlets. Nowadays, however, organically produced food has countless organic labels, which compete against each other and against many other, mostly weaker labels of VSS. The majority of consumers are confused by the spate of labels and can hardly cope with it. The bargaining power of the supermarket chains and their discriminating retailing practices put enormous pressure on the negotiations over prices and conditions. The premium payments for organic food, once the main incentive for transition for farmers, are on the decline. The more organic food moves out of the niches into mainstream food markets, the more the pioneer rents of organic innovators melt away. While the organic traders understand how to protect their profitable margins, the farmers tend to be the losers. Some of the organic labelling organizations have become big wholesalers, partly improving the sales conditions for farmers, partly being pressured by supermarkets to pass on specific requirements and purchasing conditions to farmers – the general trend however being that farmers are more and more exposed to the leverage of trading companies.[81] Other parts of the organic movement were taken over by retailers or institutional investors.[82]

5. Inherent Contradictions

That the mechanism of competition on capitalistic markets might not be compatible with IFOAM's principles of fairness, ecology, precaution and social care is not surprising. But also the intrinsic concept of labelling and certification itself might be at odds with the organic principles. The very idea to translate principles into a static global standard, to stress the notion of international equivalence, attach a label to the products, and certify the producers for their compliance is strange, because organic agriculture means to look for and apply locally adapted agronomic solutions. In contrast, 'other VSS' generally built on uniform methods of farming all over the world.[83] The label warrants a uniform quality of the product to all traders globally. It relieves the traders from potential risks through negligent and irresponsible conduct or unsafe management practices. Nevertheless, it disrespects smallholder agriculture's strength for diversity.

Organic farming stands for the opposite: Culturally the farmers should use their specific traditional knowledge (like seeds) and build their farming systems on utilizing local resources, with exceptional care for their soils and animals, their climate conditions to the utmost extend, and refrain from the temptation

---

81 The times of organic marketing by small groceries in the neighbourhood are over. In Berlin, for instance, there are about 200 special organic food shops, of which 133 call themselves Bio-Supermarket. They are bigger, run by trading companies, and have some 2–50 shops each in town. See: www.veganberlin.com/de/guide/karte-aller-bio-supermaerkte-naturkostlaeden-berlin/

82 The inflation of farm land prices on both sides of the Atlantic has attracted investment funds on their search for profit. The speculation with land fit for organic farming offers a special deal. Investments funds like Iroquois Valley, Farmland LP and Dirt Capitol buy farmland, make the transition to organic certification, and rent it to organic farmers through a lease program. The value of the organic land asset rises even more so over time, because organic farming promises to take care of the quality of the soil. The funds advertise the investment by announcing it like 'to throw money at a planet-saving project – and that's a win for everyone'. See: www.naturespath.com/en-ca/blog/organic-farming-next-big-investment-opportunity/

83 The attempt of GlobalGAP, for instance, to open up its criteria for 'national interpretations' and thus enable national GAP schemes such as KenyaGAP, ThaiGAP or IndoGAP was not very successful, because the customers of the label preferred to buy products certified under the original GlobalGAP standard.

to only substitute biological for chemical inputs. Traditional knowledge is a matter of backwardness for the commercial VSS, and they are inspired to make use of whatever new innovation increases the yields, as a pure quantitative and economies of scale narrative. In contrast, organic farming scrutinizes externally developed methods and inputs very carefully before they accept their adoption. Organic farming places utmost importance on closed nutrient cycles and closing the biological and technical loops on the farm, on soil stewardship and a resulting holistic (reproductive) concept of productivity and yields.

From an organic perspective, what must be avoided is that the regulators of the Global North define and evaluate the farming systems of the Global South with purely Northern concepts and procedures. Regulatory mechanisms are certainly needed, but they should include regional definitions and heterogeneous interpretations to take account of the special conditions of other socio-cultural environments and biophysical as well as climatic conditions. Static rules of standards will always find it very difficult to capture the richness of principles and conditions 'organic' is built upon (see Vogl et al., 2005: 1–26).

However, standards in themselves do not need complete alignment of requirements across regions and countries (a 'one-size-fits-all' approach). A requirement could be that local conventions and practices in different regions have been respected, which themselves differ between regions. This would be a holistic approach that would look at the systems around the products and not only at the products themselves. The rationale for such a holistic approach is that one needs to keep sustainable systems alive in order to ensure the future flow of products.

6. Certification

The kind of commercial certification as prevailing nowadays diverts the organic movement from its original ideas. It puts the farmers under the rule of external certifying bodies that inspect compliance by merely applying a (mechanical and often bureaucratic) check list (i.e. danger of 'ritualism') (see Squatrito et al., 2020: 19). This kind of audit does not do justice to the complex matter of 'organic', it is more an impersonal inspection than a consultation, and is a costly procedure, which causes the exclusion of many small producers. Originally the idea was to provide a verification to buyers who were at a distance from farmers. Basically however it was meant as a community-based process, emphasizing the learning part of it. IFOAM has recognized some inadequacy of 'Third Party

Certification' to its principles. Still it is under intense pressure to provide a quality assurance system like all 'other VSS'. The demand derives from the consumers, the traders and retailers, and from governments. They all ask for a trustworthy surveillance in order to maintain the integrity of organic food and agriculture.

Through the strong pressure of IFOAM member organizations from the South, IFOAM tried hard to overcome the dilemma at least partly. It is the only standard organization that has put much effort into an alternative certification process, the 'Participatory Guarantee System (PGS)',[84] achieving some success even with certain governments,[85] who recognized this 'peer report system' as a complimentary certification procedure. However neither the governments of the North nor the big supermarket chains have ever embraced PGS-schemes. The conclusion is that PGS-certified products can only be found on domestic markets in some countries. But even there, governments make it hard for the PGS-System to function, like the recent changes by the Indian Government, which introduced an extra official authentication to its recognition.

The VSS other than 'organic' also do accept alternative procedures to relax the stringent certification rules to a certain degree, like certification of a producers' group (Group Certification) with an appropriate associated 'Internal Control System', in order to facilitate smallholders' participation in standard programs and their markets. However, no 'other VSS' than 'organic' has made so much effort to advocate these alternatives, to develop tailor-made training programs and to propagate them so heavily.

But even with reforms of the certification procedure like these, the fundamental contradiction has not really been lifted: certification remains to be a barrier to participation of smallholders in the program. Previously the certification of 'organic' was mostly controlled by agencies linked to producers and close to the organic movement. With the internationalization of organic trade the process is susceptible to get captured by other vested interests following the logic of agribusiness.

---

84 PGS are locally focused quality assurance systems. They certify producers based on active participation of stakeholders and are built on a foundation of trust, social networks and knowledge exchange. They are not accredited according to ISO Guidelines or any national system.
85 From data collected in 2019, it is estimate that there are at least 223 PGS initiatives in 76 countries, with at least 567.142 producers involved and 496.104 producers certified by PGS initiatives, 57 initiatives are under development and 166 are fully operational (FiBL/IFOAM, 2019: 161).

The social principles of IFOAM (including fairness and care) are hard to put into tight criteria for making them fit for auditing purposes. Not really being part of the governmental standards on organic, they are more easily to omit or even to violate. The features by which 'organic' differs most from 'other VSS' are soft and ill-defined. To practice and propagate organic agriculture just as a chemical-free agronomic technique does not do justice to the original organic concept. It reduces the idea to a practice by which external agro-chemical inputs are replaced by natural once, just because this simple form of transition is easily auditable.

7. Conclusion

The internal contradictions of and external pressure on the organic movement have pushed 'organic' more and more into an agribusiness dependency and converts a movement that advocates system change in food and agriculture into a trade mark for individual products. That is pushing organic standards pretty close to other commercial VSS. The original hope that 'organic' might lead to a transformation of the production system in food and agriculture is fading. Individual farms might be able to escape these tendencies and traps, especially as they manage to build alliances with alternative trade initiatives, building new and tighter links between consumers and producers in order to bypass the giant supermarket chains. These kinds of initiatives actually can do without an organic label. However, the once very promising movement is at risk to lose its integrity as alternative to the agribusiness model. All the adverse forces will weaken the organic standards and will undermine arguments about the benefits of organic methods over time. The forces weakening 'organic' have only one objective: To break down barriers to make it easier for large agribusiness firms to enter the market and to increase opportunities for profit-making in lucrative organic production and marketing segments. Freyer and Bingen (2014: 290) come to the sobering conclusion that 'it is questionable whether the organic movement as defined by IFOAM's Principles could survive as model for the future. It does not fit into the political economy of today'.

II.

VSS at a Crossroads

The nascent impression that VSS had run out of steam on delivering on their aspirations and stated objectives and might therefore get into troubled future waters materialized in Mai 2017. The British retailer Sainsbury's, which once boasted that it was the world's largest retailer selling Fairtrade products, declared that its own-brand teas would no longer be certified by Fairtrade. This move was a 'bombshell' for third-party certified VSS in general, because it came from precisely those business circles that once were the initiators or staunch supporters of many VSS (for more information, see Subramanian, 2019).

Although Sainsbury's torpedo was launched at the Fairtrade standard, together with organic standards widely regarded as crown jewel of the entire VSS edifice,[1] the justification given by Sainsbury's and other globally active retailers and agro-food processing companies, such as Mondelēz and Starbucks, that followed Sainsbury's step a few months later, was of general nature on the wanting

---

1 Organic and Fairtrade standards ranked top in the evaluation of the selection of sustainability criteria and the impact appraisal of VSS. For an analysis and evaluation of the environmental, social and economic criteria used by the most important VSS to foster sustainability (see Potts et al., 2014: sections 3.5. and 3.6.).

impact of VSS when compared with the required effort and related costs for a third-party VSS certification system.

There is not only widespread 'label fatigue' among consumers, but also among large agro-food companies. They highlight, for instance, that there is one VSS that promises a carbon-free product, another a carbon-neutral one, and a third a carbon-reducing one. The more VSS there are like that, the less one knows about them – about what they stand for, and about how meaningful they are. It goes without saying that this fuels doubt in the credibility of the entire VSS system, on the one hand, and rises suspicion of 'greenwashing', on the other.

According to interviews, done by Samanth Subramanian (2019),

> several people in the corporate world offered an even more depressing version of this story: companies are sidling away from third-party certifiers because their optimistic project – the idea that the market can be heedful of its own abuses and correct itself – has, in a grand sense, failed. After decades of work, these certifiers have been unable to truly alter the imbalance in global trade; they have struggled [yet failed] to protect farmers, or to arm them for their various social, economic and environmental battles.

And Subramanian continues that

> the proof is in the dire projections for the future of farming, showing how vanishing agricultural biodiversity, the warming climate and the ageing and impoverishment of farmers are all endangering the world's crops – which means they are also endangering the supply chains of companies who rely upon farmers in Asia, Africa and Latin America to manufacture chocolate bars, coffee pods, or cotton T-shirts.

The alternative approach now being pursued by the big agro-food processing, trading and marketing companies is however unlikely to alter the situation and effectively deal with some of the root causes. Third-party certification is being replaced by in-house programs to source sustainably grown produce, which stand on the shoulders of massive investment in corporate capacity-building programs, but also payments of 'strategic or loyalty premiums' (e.g. in Starbucks' CAFE Practices, Mondelēz's Cocoa Life or Nestlé's Cocoa Plan programmes) to dedicated producers. However, these self-certification schemes are one-sided as their criteria and assessment methods are unilaterally defined by the corporate players although, given the severe crises in agriculture, the companies are undoubtedly motivated to protect farms and farm workers – if only to secure their own future profits.[2]

Another manifestation of the crisis VSS find themselves in are the recent calls by several of the largest cocoa and chocolate companies for an EU due diligence regulation. Also the European umbrella associations for cocoa (ECA) and chocolate (Caobisco) have issued statements supporting a due diligence regulation. There are three principal reasons for industry support for regulation: firstly, the due diligence principles, outlined by the OECD (see Section III.A.4) provide a level of clarity and certainty. Secondly, a mandatory regulation would level the playing field, requiring all competitors to operate according to the same principles; corporations could no longer compete through facilitating, committing or ignoring human rights abuses or environmental degradation. Thirdly, it would allow for more impact through higher ambitions and more joined efforts (Fountain and Huetz-Adams, 2020b: 15–16).

A. What Are the Key Market Challenges, What Can VSS Realistically Deliver and Where Must They Fail?

Any form of sustainable agriculture that does not improve the economic and social conditions of producers, including guaranteeing a sufficient living wage or income for a decent life, is bound to lose farmers' interest, discourage their efforts in environmental protection and run the risk of falling apart sooner or later. As Fountain and Huetz-Adams (2018: 13) point out in the Cocoa Barometer 2018, 'a value chain that accepts structural poverty as inevitable can never be called sustainable'.

To illustrate the extent of the drama on lacking economic sustainability and living income[3] for VSS-certified producers let us briefly give an overview of the

---

2 For more information on the 'in-house' certification programs of some of the key corporate players, see Subramanian (2019).
3 Living Income is the net annual income required for a household in a particular place to afford a decent standard of living for all members of that household. Elements of a decent standard

situation for cocoa farmers in West Africa, drawing on reported figures for the 2018–2019 harvest and projections for the 2020–2021 harvest.[4] The situation for Côte d'Ivoire and Ghana[5] can be summarized as follows[6]:

	US$/MT	Percentage of living income
Price for conventional cocoa at farm gate	1,145	36
Guaranteed floor farm gate price by CCC and Cocobod[7] for 2020–2021 harvest:	1,840	58
Oxfam Fairtrade flexible premium	2,668	85
Fairtrade Living Income Reference Price	2,400	76
Recent price range of Rainforest Alliance	1,300–1,500	44
Required living income as estimated by Fairtrade and Coco Barometer	3,100–3,200[8]	100[9]

of living include: food, water, housing, education, health care, transport, clothing, and other essential needs including provision for unexpected events (Living Income, 2020).

4 It is estimated that cocoa production provides livelihoods for some 14 million rural workers on big plantations and for a further 2.5 million small-scale farmers.

5 Côte d'Ivoire and Ghana account for about 43 and 20 percent of global cocoa production in recent years. Compare: International Cocoa Organisation, ICCO Quarterly Bulletin of Cocoa Statistics.

6 Figures derived from Cocoa Barometer (2020), VOICE Network (2019a), and VOICE Network (2019b).

7 Ivorian Conseil du Café-Cacao (CCC) and Ghana Cocoa Board (Cocobod).

8 In a research paper for the Cocoa Barometer 2020, Fountain and Huetz-Adams (2020a) calculated a level of 'living income' from cocoa that should be at least US$3,166/MT for Côte d'Ivoire, and US$3,116/MT for Ghana.

9 In July 2019, the governments of Ghana and Côte d'Ivoire introduced a US$400/MT living income differential (LID) surcharge for all cocoa bean sales of the 2020–2021 season. Côte d'Ivoire and Ghana plan to use funds raised from the LID to guarantee farmers get 70 percent of a US$2,600/MT fob target price. If global prices rise above US$2,900/MT, proceeds from the LID will be placed in a stabilization fund that would be used to ensure farmers get the target price when market prices fall (Reuters, 2019). As Fountain and Huetz-Adams (2020b: 22) correctly point out, however, intervening on price without looking at supply measures and enabling policies to develop a healthy cocoa sector may not have the desired positive impact in the long term.

The table above provides a self-evident, yet sober picture. VSS-certified prices are falling far short of the required price level for guaranteeing a sufficient living income level for farmers. Even Oxfam's and Fairtrade's offered prices are falling some 15–25 percent short of the price level required for a living income. What is more, not all VSS-certified cocoa is sold as certified with a certain price premium; depending on the standard, in recent years between 40 and 80 percent of certified cocoa has been sold as conventional one (Fountain and Huetz-Adams, 2018: 40). Though the average income of VSS-certified farmers might be slightly higher than non-certified farmers, the overall impact is relatively low; a certified farmer is still nowhere near earning a living income (VOICE Network, 2019a). There is thus[10] a significant gap between the level of poverty alleviation consumers think they are contributing to, and the reality on the cocoa farms.[11]

There is little doubt that the most disturbing human rights violations and ecological disturbances have a causal link to the completely unsatisfactory living income level of cocoa farmers. A recent documentary, based on an extensive series of interviews with cocoa farmers and farm workers in Côte d'Ivoire, provides evidence on massive use of child slaves that illegally entered the country mostly from neighbouring Burkina Faso, as well as the illegal logging and use for cocoa farming of tropical rain forest. Virtually all interviewed farmers emphasized that they would stop illegal logging and use of child labour and send children to school if cocoa farm-gate prices were guaranteeing a sufficient living income.[12] In 2001 the key cocoa trading and processing companies agreed to phase out child labour, non-existing minimum wages and deforestation. However, it is a sobering and disconcerting fact that 20 years later this objective remains largely unfulfilled (ZDFInfo Doku, 2020).

---

10 Buntzel and Mari aptly describe this situation of VSS-compliant farmers as 'a bit less poor' (Buntzel and Mari, 2016: 229).

11 In Côte d'Ivoire, even of the certified farmers only 12 percent earned a living income in 2018 (Fountain and Huetz-Adams, 2020b: 39).

12 Although the share of VSS-certified cocoa production area has meanwhile surpassed one quarter of total cocoa acreage, according to a paper of NORC at the University of Chicago, the use of child labour on cocoa farms in Ghana and Côte d'Ivoire has increased by an estimated 13 percent since 2008. (Sadhu et al., 2020).

Box 6: Much more sustainable cocoa production is possible – The example of FAIRAFRIC

Fairafric is a German start-up company, founded in 2016, which aims to bring about real change and create jobs that increase African income from cocoa production manifold. While initiatives like Fairtrade, UTZ or Rainforest Alliance give the impression of moving millions of farmers out of poverty, the picture on the ground looks different – a couple of percent more income on almost nothing is still almost nothing. While price premiums paid by Faitrade are about US$240 per ton or some 10 percent of the international cocoa price, by UTZ (some US$100 or some 5 percent) and Rainforest Alliance (no premium), the price premium provided by Fairafric to cocoa farmers is US$600 (almost 30 percent of the international cocoa price).

However, Fairafric goes well beyond the limits of fair trade. The company's approach lifts Ghana's income per ton of cocoa from some US$2,000 (conventional) or US$2,400 (Fairtrade) to more than US$10,000 and creates valuable, desperately needed jobs outside of farm work by turning cocoa into ready for export chocolate products made in Ghana. The daily minimum wage in Ghana is 10.65 Cedis, which translates into a monthly salary of approximately US$55. At Fairafric's solar-powered organic chocolate factory in rural Suhum, the monthly intermediate salary is 6.4 times the Ghanaian minimum wage, approximately US$352. Apart from the distinctly higher salary level, Fairafric's employees also profit from a good number of other social and occupational benefits, such as safe clothing, free health care, free staff transport, subsidized lunch, temperature-controlled work-space, and company pension plan.

Intermediate salary:
6,4 times the
Ghanaian minimum wage

36-hour week
4 days, 9 hours

13th month's salary

Weekend work is
payed extra

Paid overtime

HELINA
Chocolatiere
in training

As a result, the average share of the cocoa producing country in the retail price of most chocolate products is around 6 percent (conventional) or 7–8 percent for fairtrade-certified cocoa products. Under Fairafric's approach, cocoa farmers and chocolate producers in Ghana obtain roughly a one third share of the retail price of chocolate products in export markets. This results in an income increase in Ghana of 400 percent compared to conventional chocolate production in Europe, for which cocoa beans are exported, but not processed in the countries of cocoa origin.

In a nutshell, Fairafric has intentionally decided to stay away from Fairtrade schemes, because the company wants to make consumers aware that one should not only trade resources fairly, but that countries like Ghana should have the chance to make something out of their abundant natural wealth so to escape poverty by themselves.

Compiled from information available at: https://fairafric.com/en/home/ and the press kit at: http://fairafric.com/en/press/ (accessed on 8 March 2021)

What explains then the lackluster progress and weak role of VSS in improving the economic and social sustainability of farmers?

Fountain and Huetz-Adams (2018: 28–29) in the Cocoa Barometer 2018 come to the following bottom line:

> Almost all of the current efforts to increase farmer income are based on technical solutions (increased production, crop diversification, use of agrochemicals and new planting material, increased efforts to improve farming techniques). However, the challenges facing the cocoa sector – and almost all other commodities as well – are often not technical, but deal with power and political economy, such as price formation, the asymmetrical bargaining power of farmers, unbridled market concentration of multinationals, and a lack of transparency and accountability ... Tackling political problems with technical solutions will not foster a sustainable cocoa sector, but simply install another form of a business-as-usual scenario.

Against the background of this conclusion, let us identify and analytically go through the most important systemic issues that constrain or nullify the role and impact of VSS.

1. The Asymmetrical Market Power along the Supply Chain

For cocoa, for instance, the value of the final product that reaches farmers is small and has been shrinking over the years. On average, farmers receive only between 3 and 7 percent of the retail price of a chocolate bar, compared to up to 50 percent in the 1970s and 16 percent in the 1980s. By comparison, the chocolate brand manufacturers capture about 40 percent of the price and retailers some 35 percent. Market concentration at each step of the supply and processing chain is very high. Barry Callebaut (Switzerland), Cargill (US) and Olam (Singapore) account for about 60 percent of world cocoa processing, and Mars (US), Nestlé (Switzerland), Mondelez (US), Hershey's (US), Ferrero (Italy) and Lindt (Switzerland) account for 40 percent of the global consumer chocolate market (Brack, 2019: 10–11).

Generally, the market concentration at each step in global food supply chains is very high. As can be seen from Figure 4, only few companies account for the lion's share of sales at each step.

Figure 4: Market concentration in global food supply chains

Input & Services	Farming	Trade & Processing	Food Manufacturing	Retail & Marketing
Three Conglomerates dominate nearly 60% of global turnover for commercial seed and agricultural chemicals* **60%**	**The Vast Majority** of the world's farms are small-scale and family farms **1%** But 1% of farms in the world are larger than 50 hectares and they control 65% of the world's agricultural land	**Four Companies** account for 70% of trade in agricultural commodities globally by revenue** **70%** e.g. wheat, corn and soybeans	**50 Food Manufacturers** account for half of all global food sales	In the European Union: **10** **Just Ten Supermarkets** account for over half of all food retail sales

Notes: * Bayer-Monsanto, Dupont-Dow, and Chem-China Syngenta; ** Archer Daniels Midland (ADM), Bunge, Cargill, and Louis Dreyfus Co.
Source: Based on Oxfam (2018: 38).

This general power imbalance is also mirrored in the appropriation of price premiums or quality bonuses that are envisaged in some VSS schemes.[13] Generally the appropriation structure of the premiums follows that of the current patterns of added value in the supply chain. In other words, cocoa farmers tend to receive only about 10 percent or even less of any additional premium Cent paid by the final consumer of chocolate products. Studies on the sales margins of supermarkets for various organic products relative to the margins for conventional produce in Germany, for instance, show that there is a considerable difference, ranging from 39 percent for organic cheese (relative to 25 percent for conventional) to 61 percent for organic chicken (compared to 39 percent for conventional) (Berner, 2019).

In other words, VSS-compliant products are a lucrative business opportunity for food processors, traders and retailers, but poor farmers, who would need most the extra income paid by consumers profit least (Berner, 2019). And that would undoubtedly have to change, if VSS are to contribute to true sustainability. As Figure 5 however highlights, in recent decades farmers have lost most ground in value added along food supply chains. Whereas farmers' share in retail prices shrank by 13 percent, it increased by 11.5 percent for supermarkets.

Figure 5: Changes in the share of end consumer prices between the principal supply chain actors in the period 1995–2011 in percent

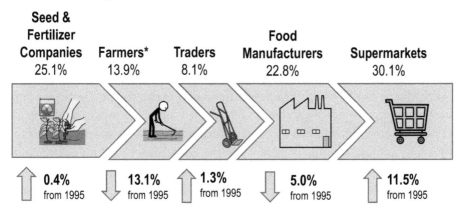

Seed & Fertilizer Companies	Farmers*	Traders	Food Manufacturers	Supermarkets
25.1%	13.9%	8.1%	22.8%	30.1%
0.4% from 1995	13.1% from 1995	1.3% from 1995	5.0% from 1995	11.5% from 1995

Note: Data at the global aggregate level. * Small' and large-scale.
Source: Based on Oxfam (2018: 17).

13 As mentioned before, B2B VSS do normally not provide for price premiums. Their bait is access to large markets.

Another source of concern is the use of restrictive business and trade practices by the large corporations in the supply chain, especially large retailers. A recent survey of food chain suppliers in the EU found that 96 percent of interviewed suppliers had been subject to at least one form of unfair practice. They include unfair practices on sourcing strategy (playing off one supplier against another), contractual terms (systemic absence of written contracts, short-term contracts, insufficient lead times on orders or declining the acceptance of shipments for quality reasons at times of oversupply), pricing and payment structure (delays in payments to suppliers to increase margins, deductions or unexpected changes faced by suppliers) or demanding fees from suppliers (charges for customer complaints, fees for marketing campaigns/promotion). The impact of such practices has been to depress prices paid to producers/suppliers and to increase the risks – for example, of failed harvests, climate disruptions or increases in the costs of production – which they have to absorb (see EU, 2019 and Oxfam, 2018: 41).

2. The Race to the Bottom

The cost-treadmill effect, which was briefly outlined in Box 5, is bound to favour those producers that are best prepared and resourced for meeting the VSS requirements at the lowest up front and running costs. Furthermore, as the competition among VSS schemes intensifies, one can observe a sort of standard drift towards those VSS that have less demanding and stringent requirements. As already mentioned, an analysis of the standard drift phenomenon by the University of Muenster in Germany for the case of VSS-certified coffee found that about 60 percent of certified coffee available in the market is certified by VSS at the lower end of the standard rating, whereas only approximately 34 percent of the total volume of certified coffee adheres to VSS on the higher end. This indicates that there is a relative race to the bottom occurring in the sector as VSS-certified coffee increases its market share (TransSustain, 2019). Gibbon argues that such schemes water down standards on Fairtrade, confuse consumers by blurring the boundaries between Fairtrade and non-Fairtrade products, load the costs of compliance onto producers while giving little back in the shape of price premiums. Many VSS schemes are skewed heavily toward estate production, with little attention to smallholders, and more generally add to standards proliferation (Gibbon, 2004, cited in Green, 2005).[14]

---

14 The recent in-depth study of the Changing Markets Foundation (2018) on VSS schemes in palm oil and textiles production as well as fisheries comes to the same conclusion.

3. Limited Control over a Range of Essential Flanking and Supportive Elements for VSS

To function effectively, VSS require a supportive legal, economic, technical, social and infrastructural framework in producing countries. Most of these elements are also of key importance to farmers' livelihoods, such as access to social infrastructure like schools or health care as well as appropriate technical facilities, such as roads or information technology. Besides, VSS often require testing laboratories, accredited according to ISO Guidelines, and the existence of a skilled food safety authority as well as public extension services.

More broadly, land and forest governance, land use and land enforcement (including land tenure systems or inheritance regime) as well as supportive financial services and credit systems have significant impacts on the conditions of farmers and their ability to implement VSS. Yet, most of these elements and factors are the responsibilities of government and are difficult for external stakeholders to influence.

As already mentioned above, there is a certain risk that VSS-inspired changes in such national policies and support measures may result in a crowding out of scarce public resources being devoted to other more urgent development tasks, in particular food security or infant mortality.

4. The Myth of Yield Increases

One of the key illusions of many VSS programmes and associated support activities on fostering best management practice is the assumption that by jacking up farmers' productivity their welfare would improve in tandem. Many activities of donors, the private sector and NGOs therefore focus on identifying best farming and management practice and organizing training and capacity-building events on teaching other producers to emulate best farming and management practice. This includes the appropriate use of agro-chemicals (often with the direct and indirect involvement of large agro-chemical companies) for improving plant protection, new planting material, the use of more intelligent or smart-farming techniques as well as the application of remote sensing and big data to optimize yields. With the exception of organic agriculture and partly also Fairtrade, most other efforts of boosting yields are done in the classical way, i.e. by promoting a one-sided and linear productivity drive, based on an external (agro-chemical) input-intensive production model for maximizing the harvest of a particular crop, in many cases a mono-crop.

A significant challenge in boosting productivity however is to do it sustainably and not based on 'resource-mining'. There is also the need to redefine productivity. However, it is not sufficient to theoretically redefine productivity; one also needs to redesign the economic system that has created a distorted view of what is productive and what is not. Today, productivity is measured by how many trees one person can cut down with a chainsaw or how much fish a fisherman can scoop up from the sea (i.e. labour productivity). However, as natural resources dwindle, the real productivity lies in how these resources re-generate.[15] In reality, one is productive if there is more forest next year than today, if there are more fish and if the soil becomes more fertile by the years instead of being exhausted and eroded. Similarly, we are more productive if the food we produce and consume is healthy rather than if it is cheap.[16] This is the rational for the suggestion to define the term as 'integral productivity', which integrates economic with social, cultural and ecological components (see Haerlin et al., 2018). Such productivity concept measures the productivity (labour productivity and resource efficiency) of a regenerative production system, including diversification of production, soil, ground water and landscape stewardship.

The present linear, one-sided approach on boosting productivity is part of a micro-economic approach that improves the yield (a harvested crop per hectare) of a particular farmer, often in combination with reducing production costs, relative to another farmer, leading to an improved competitive position as supplier. While this appears to be an essential step and achievement at producer level, contrary to the popular belief among many circles, this is not a panacea that will resolve the problem of lacking economic and social sustainability of VSS-certified producers.

---

15 This is marked every year by the Earth Overshoot Day, which calculates the illustrative calendar date on which the planet's resource consumption for the year exceeds the earth's capacity to regenerate those resources that year.

16 As correctly emphasized by Rundgren (2015: 241), 'productivity in farming can be measured in many ways: per area unit; per person-hour; per unit of deployed capital; per energy input or; per water unit. The comparisons can consider total biological production, ecosystem services or only what is directly useful to human being in the form of food, fibre and fuel . . .. We can also ask if the productivity is serving to maintain the productive resources or if it is based on extraction of non-renewable resources, resources which perhaps were abundant but now are increasingly scarce. Can we even talk about productivity if the production is based on the unsustainable use of irrigation, fossil fuel and soil management practices which erode the soil? . . .. "Productivity" can have a completely different meaning if we counted the impact on ecosystems and the external costs caused by farming.'

Assuming that the total consumption volume of the crop in question remains largely unchanged, productivity improvements at company level will increase total (macro-economic and global) production volume that may depress international prices. While the specific farmer with a higher productivity improves his competitive position, he/she will not gain in a direct proportional way, because oversupply will shave away part of the productivity-induced income gains or even more.

For the case of cocoa, for instance, where there has been considerable oversupply in recent years, according to the Cocoa Barometer 2018 (Fountain and Huetz-Adams, 2018: 46),

> increasing yields offers a window of opportunity to decrease areas planted with cocoa trees. These areas might be converted to diversified crops or be converted back to natural forests to restore biodiversity and roll back some of the adverse effects of deforestation.

5. *Economic and Social Sustainability Remain Illusionary without Reforming the International Commodity Price-Fixing System*

As can be seen from the recent development of international cocoa prices (Figure 6), while large cocoa processing companies have invested millions of dollars in VSS-projects in recent years, their purchasing departments have saved roughly US$1,000 per tonne of cocoa due to the price decline. According to the Cocoa Barometer 2018, this adds up to approximately US$4.7 billion of reduced purchasing costs in the 2017–2018 harvest season compared to the previous year alone. Even senior industry representatives admit that the price decline of cocoa will de facto erase all the sustainability gains that have been achieved in the past ten years (Fountain and Huetz-Adams, 2018: 11).

Figure 6: Long-term trend of international cocoa prices in real terms for the period 1952 to 2020 (in thousands 2018 US$ per tonne)

Source: Fountain, Huetz-Adams (2020b: 50), based on LMC International (2020)

Since the liberalization of many commodity markets in the second half of the 1980s, international prices have been fixed at the futures market. These price fixings are then taken as reference price for supply contracts between commodity producers and purchasers. Commodity exchanges are also a playground for speculators, in particular at times of volatile prices thereby exacerbating volatility. In sum and with the benefit of hindsight, derivatives at commodity exchanges have proved unsuitable for addressing long-term price instability (for most agricultural commodities, coverage is generally restricted to a few months) and they cannot maintain higher prices for sellers (Green, 2005: 24). Thus, prices are still determined by lead firms with little or no collective action ability by lower tier suppliers in the supply chain.

Although corporate agents can make some price-lifting or stabilization interventions, they all tend to reinforce oversupply and put future pressure on the price level. It is most likely far more effective that governments in producing countries are conducting a more coherent agricultural policy, setting the right incentives and disincentives as well as providing appropriate extension services and investment in diversifying production patterns. In parallel, there is the need for developing some level of national and international supply management, in which producing country governments must play a more pro-active role. As pointed out by the Cocoa Barometer 2018 (Fountain and Huetz-Adams, 2018: 54), at both national and global levels, this would require the establishment of workable mechanisms for (re)allocating individual production rights, monitoring quality and production methods, overcoming rent seeking, corruption and tax avoidance, workable mechanisms for monitoring national production and trade, (re)allocating production rights between countries, and overcoming free rider problems (for a more elaborate discussion of national and international supply coordination see the next chapter).

To put this in perspective, according to calculations by Daviron and Ponte, Fairtrade coffee sales (offering the highest farm gate prices of all VSS-schemes) returned between 12 and 21 percent of the retail price to the producer cooperatives in the early 2000s. Even the higher end of this spectrum was only what farmers achieved in the mainstream market in the 1970s and 1980s under the International Coffee Agreement (cited in Green, 2005: 27).

6. Summing up

After almost three decades of efforts to make VSS work and widespread experience with them one must realistically conclude that VSS, as a business-related perspective on sustainability that works through the supply chain, have not triggered a large-scale sustainability transformation of markets through a continuously expanding market share of VSS-compliant products. Up to now, they create more an illusion of progress than full-sector, i.e. transformational change. As Glasbergen concluded (2018: 250),

> perhaps the most important effect of private sustainability standards has been awareness raising on sustainability issues and not turning the market around.

Moreover, Glasbergen continues that

> we face a well-known paradox here: we cannot do without the market, but the market on its own will not be able to bring about large scale sustainable system change, better economic prospects, and empowerment of the millions of smallholders in agriculture.

The authors of the recurrent Cocoa Barometer (VOICE Network, 2019a) come to a similar conclusion:

> It is time to realize that the cocoa farmer is not the problem; the problem is systemic. Systemic problems require systemic solutions, not a tick-box exercise at

farm level [such as under VSS]. Currently, the cocoa farmer bears almost all of the risk, reaps hardly any of the reward, and no one is taking the responsibility for this systemic failure . . .. The systemic failure of voluntary initiatives gives strong evidence that legislative measures on ecological and human rights due diligence are needed. In the meantime, all standard setting organizations need to improve their systems, acknowledging that a sustainable solution needs to include price mechanisms.

Is There Any Future Perspective for VSS and What Might It Look Like?

As already pointed out above, VSS and the endeavour to improve the functioning of their standard systems have largely become an end in themselves. An increasing share of VSS-compliant products in global markets is anything but an indication for overcoming the key systemic problems of agro-food markets that would usher into transformational change. If VSS are to play any constructive role for a trans-formation of the agro-food supply chains towards truly sustainable conditions, they would have to be part of a systemic and holistic approach that primarily relies on regulation and a pro-active regulatory role, complemented by voluntary initiatives that go a step further than the regulatory floor. As pointed out in the previous chapter, most of the sector-wide efforts in many agro-food commodities have almost exclusively focused on technical solutions to jack up productivity. However, the key challenges facing agro-food producers are not technical, but concern power and political economy, such as price formation, the asymmetrical bargaining power of farmers, unbridled market concentration of multinationals, and a lack of transparency and accountability (for more detail, see Fountain and Huetz-Adams, 2018: 28–29).

This part of the manuscript will therefore deal with necessities and options to tackle the key systemic problems in agri-food supply chains and review, within this very context, opportunities for a constructive role of VSS to contribute to true sustainability. It builds on the analysis of the most important systemic issues that constrain or nullify the role and impact of VSS made in part II of the manuscript.

A. Rebalancing Power in Global Agri-food Supply Chains

To counter the asymmetrical market power of large agro-food processing, trading and retail companies and to strengthen the bargaining power of producers, there is a need for action on several fronts:

- improving national coordination of production;
- rebalancing power in global supply chains: strengthening and changing the focus of competition policy;
- limiting the scope for using restrictive or unfair business and trading practices; and
- improving monitoring and transparency in international supply chains for avoiding precarious employment conditions, infringement of human rights, and environmental damage (i.e. due diligence).

While reviewing these tools it is important to bear in mind that various individual measures, such as establishing minimum prices or wages for farmers or improving monitoring and transparency must go hand-in-hand with efforts to address the market forces that relentlessly squeeze value from producers (i.e. improved bargaining positions of producers and international supply management). An integral part of that endeavour will be a more important role of public governance.

1. Restoration of National Supply Management: State or Producer Organization Driven

The structural adjustment programmes of the IMF and related country loan programmes of the World Bank in the 1980s and 1990s phased out many state-led supply coordination and support structures in developing countries, in particular in sub-Saharan Africa, through the abolition of state marketing boards, cut-backs in sources of finance and sharp reductions in technical assistance programmes. Commodity marketing boards played a key role in the development of the agricultural export sectors in many African countries and the policy of dismantling them[1] has been widely criticized. Apart from their role in stabilizing prices, they were necessary for providing ancillary services, such as extension and rural infrastructure, including input provision, product distribution services and credit. The destruction of the national marketing boards considerably reduced the capacity of farmers to raise their share in value chain rents by removing a useful intermediary that could improve farmers' bargaining power with large corporate buyers at a time, when the international markets for agricultural commodities have become much more concentrated (see Green, 2005: 4–5).

National marketing boards also used to play a vital role in building a globally recognized national quality standard. Such territorial reputations were built on local specificities of climate, soil etc., but marketing boards ensured consistency in sorting, grading and description, and applied sanctions when these standards were violated. National reputations established in this way attracted premiums for growers of higher quality products (see Gibbon, 2003).

FAO's State of Agricultural Commodity Markets' report (FAO, 2004) emphasizes that

> now that the boards are gone, in many cases neither government nor the private sector has taken on these roles. Smallholders in many developing countries have been confronted by loss of access to credit and soaring prices for inputs. Poor market infrastructure and information channels leave them vulnerable to price volatility and exploitation by trading companies that have often stepped in to replace the state monopoly with a private one. At the same time, public expenditures in agriculture have dwindled. In many countries, both yields and quality of commodities have fallen since the marketing boards were abolished.

With the advent of supermarkets and their supply chains, private quality control and assurance systems emerged that bypassed or replaced that of national commodity boards.

For marketing boards, the government would normally set an annual price at which it would purchase the commodity through intermediaries (cooperatives or licensed traders), who were given a fixed margin.[2] Such marketing boards are not

---

1 Marketing boards were dismantled in most African countries in the wake of liberalization of national economies and international trade and investment. The justification for that often was that, 'marketing boards developed reputations for being institutions of egregious inefficiency that exploited farmers and discouraged agricultural production as well as for reasons of alleged inefficiency, linked to excessive bureaucracies and corruption' (Opeyemi Ayinde, 2014).

2 It should not go without comment that this practice is severely restricted by the WTO Agreement on Agriculture – this is what the discussions on Public Stockholding programmes

limited to developing countries, but have also existed for long in some developed countries, e.g. the Australian and Canadian Wheat Boards. *Caisse de stabilisation* systems differed in that although they controlled export contracts they did not handle, export or acquire physical ownership of the commodity in question: primary processing, marketing and exporting were performed by cooperatives, private traders or state enterprises. Marketing boards and *caisses de stabilisation* had the advantage that farmers knew the price they would receive at harvest.[3] By aggregating the output of a large number of small producers, they also strengthened their bargaining power relative to buyers (UNCTAD, 2003).

Apart from state-run supply management schemes, there are also successful examples of producer organization initiatives in post-liberalization situations where the role of the state remains constrained.[4] In this regard, however, the scale and organizational model affect the benefits that accrue to farmers. The FNC, the Colombian National Coffee Growers' Federation, for instance, claims about half a million members with an average of 2 ha of coffee each. FNC operates an extension service with over 800 staff, as well as its own agricultural colleges and a research and development centre. It runs a price stabilization scheme and has diversified downstream into freeze-drying and own label sales (Green, 2005: 4–5). Cooperative groups allow farmers to aggregate their produce, supporting marketing and a stronger bargaining position with buyers. They also support the sharing of risks and a stronger negotiating position to purchase inputs such as fertilizers or crop-protection products, thus reducing costs.

have been about. Minimum prices are seen as the most egregious form of trade-distorting subsidy in the edifice of the Agreement on Agriculture.

3 The system however also had some key weaknesses. As experience from India shows: (i) minimum purchasing prices are often fixed too low; and (ii) auctions do not start with the state-fixed minimum price but below. In periods of oversupply, the price can only be buffered by public intervention purchases or supply needs to be limited by production quotas.

4 In Canada, for instance, five supply management organizations – Egg Farmers of Canada (EFC), Turkey Farmers of Canada (TFC), Chicken Farmers of Canada (CFC), the Canadian Hatching Egg Producers (CHEP) and the Ottawa-based Canadian Dairy Commission (CDC), a Crown corporation – in collaboration with provincial and national governing agencies, organizations and committees, administer the supply management system. In the dairy industry, the supply management system implements the federated provincial policy through the Canadian Milk Supply Management Committee (CMSMC), CDC, three regional milk pools – Newfoundland's, the five eastern province (P5) and four western provinces – and provincial milk marketing boards. Since 1970, the CMSMC has set the yearly national industrial raw milk production quota or Market Sharing Quota (MSQ) and the MSQ share for each province to ensure Canada to match production with domestic need and to remain self-sufficient in milk fat (Heminthavong, 2015).

In some cases, producer cooperatives can be quite big. The producer-led Kaira District Cooperative Milk Producers Chain in India (popularly known as Amul) is jointly owned by 3.6 million milk producers in Gujurat, with a sales turnover of about one billion US dollars in 2018–2019 (www.amuldairy.com/index.php/the-organization/an-overview).

Oxfam commissioned analysis suggests that small-scale farmers benefit from much higher shares of the end consumer price – around 26 percent – where they are organized in producers' organizations, which can achieve economies of scale up to the point of export, compared with those who are not and retain only around 4 percent (Oxfam, 2018: 81).

Whether a return to state marketing boards is either desirable or feasible is a moot point. However, strengthening the production capacity and bargaining position of smallholders may require an enhanced role of the state in contrast to the generally deregulatory and market-based approaches in recent decades. In this regard, it is vital that governments of producing countries do not replicate past mistakes,[5] but equip poor producers to engage with the market on more beneficial terms. As Green correctly points out (Green, 2005: 34),

> it is hard to argue on political or developmental grounds against a focus on producer organization, supported by the state in an enabling role. The hard question is, can it work? How can producer organizations become a significant counterweight in an ever-more unbalanced supply chain? How can producer organizations counter the many pressures that are steadily squeezing small-scale producers out of all but the most sluggish backwaters of international trade?

From Ecuador to Côte d'Ivoire and Thailand, several governments have moved to reintroduce minimum producer prices for crops like bananas, cocoa and rice. According to Oxfam analysis, where governments have intervened in this way, small-scale farmers receive a share of the end consumer price that is (for a basket of 12 reviewed commodities) around twice as high as that received by farmers without such support (Oxfam, 2018: 77–78). However, the system is not perfectly functioning, as national and international traders often try to undermine set price levels and rent-seeking in the public sector is not rare. Furthermore,

---

5 Such mistakes include, for instance, the difficulty in trying to limit production at a time when expanding supply was largely driven by increasing productivity. There was also a lack of enforcement mechanisms and the free-rider problem. The impact of developed country farm subsidy policies also played a role in competing commodities, such as cotton (see Green, 2005: 5).

countries with a small market share in export markets may also not be able to influence global prices, which either makes the market to collapse or leaves the government to step in to cover the difference. In sum, without effective supply management minimum prices are difficult and costly to maintain.

2. Strengthening and Changing the Focus of Competition Policy

Another area of pro-active policy making and intervention is to review, clarify or amend competition law in agro-food consuming and producing countries to address low prices paid to farmers as well as to check the accumulation and misuse of market power.[6]

A study by the Fairtrade Foundation on the grocery sector in the UK concluded that competition law was rightly designed to protect consumers from price fixing and other harmful practices. However, unless farmers and workers receive higher incomes and wages, the medium to long-term supply of commodities such as cocoa and bananas would be put at risk by lack of sufficient farm workers and the worsening impacts of climate change. These impacts will ultimately harm UK consumers, raising retail prices and even potentially compromising the nation's food supply chains.

The study further suggested that while companies did not perceive any regulatory barriers to collaborative discussions on issues such as child labour, deforestation or low productivity, they strongly felt that competition law placed severe constraints on discussions about low farmer incomes and wages. Due to the close relationship between incomes and prices, discussions on low farm-gate prices and farmer incomes were a highly sensitive issue that often led businesses to preclude any discussion on the subject whatsoever. Interviewees for the Fairtrade study described situations in which they had felt obliged to cite strict disclaimers at the beginning of meetings forbidding any reference to prices in the supply chain, or where other companies had refused to attend meetings on the topic, citing competition law risks. Overall, they felt that there was very limited space to discuss even pre-competitive efforts to address low farm-gate prices. Interviewees called for more precise guidance on current rules, and a more supportive policy environment, to help unblock the barriers to progress they were experiencing (Long, 2017: 37–38).

---

6 More effective competition laws and policies could also be supplemented by, or to some extent even replaced by the setting of minimum basic prices within agricultural policy for each commodity. But that policy option has been a major issue of contention within the WTO.

According to Oxfam, in Europe and the US, the use of competition or anti-trust legislation has diminished over the past three decades. Furthermore, any application of competition laws has largely focused on the protection of consumers rather than the abuse of power in other parts of the supply chain (Oxfam, 2018: 46). The strengthening of national and international competition law[7] could rebalance power in global supply chains, but only if it shifts from its current focus on consumer welfare and retail prices (i.e. monopoly/oligopoly) to one on producers and farm gate prices (monopsony/oligopsony). Improved monitoring and transparency efforts, for instance, through the revival of the defunct UN Centre on Transnational Corporations would be insufficient. However, the UN's recent work and activities on the role of competition policy in promoting sustainable and inclusive growth can offer room for more concrete and promising approaches (UNCTAD, 2015).

3. Reducing the Abuse of Power: Limiting the Use of Restrictive Business and Trading Practices

There is an array of restrictive or unfair business and trading practices used by large food processors and retailers to depress prices paid to commodity producers and increase their risks. These concern contractual terms, pricing and payment conditions as well as fees demanded from suppliers (for an overview of such practices see Oxfam, 2018: 101–102).

The European Commission has recently developed legislation to curtail the use of unfair trading practices in EU food supply chains as well as banning certain practices (EU Directive 2019/633 of 17 April 2019 on unfair trading practices in business-to-business relationships in the agricultural and food supply chain, which is foreseen to become effective by 1 November 2021).[8] The Directive enables small and medium-sized food producers, producer organizations, other organizations of suppliers and associations of such organizations, wherever they are based, to anonymously complain about abusive practices of large European buyers.

---

7 Moving it to WTO would not help – competition law there would mean that governments should not discriminate against foreign players (i.e. not positive discrimination for local small and medium-sized enterprises).

8 Available at: https://eur-lex.europa.eu/legal-content/EN/TXT/PDF/?uri= CELEX: 32019L 0633&from=en

According to Oxfam suggestions (Oxfam, 2018: 97), any legislation to prevent unfair business and trading practices

> should clearly outline access to redress for supply chain actors globally if they are directly or indirectly impacted by unfair trading practices. Enforcement mechanisms should include dissuasive sanctions and support own-initiative investigations, anonymous complaints procedures and guarantee true confidentiality.

The EU Directive makes a big step in this direction. It does however not apply to imports. It would therefore be a constructive move if the scope were broadened and thus included in future Trade and Sustainable Development chapters of EU free trade agreements.

In the past, work and intergovernmental discussions on restrictive business and trade practices were part of the work of the defunct UN Centre on Transnational Corporations and UNCTAD incorporated the subject in dialogue on competition law.

4. Legislation on due Diligence for Avoiding Precarious Employment Conditions, Infringement of Human Rights, and Environmental Damage

A recent legislative development is the promulgation of due diligence regulation that places a general requirement on large corporations to exercise due diligence in respect of human rights' and labour abuses as well as environmental harm in all their operations and supply chains.

Prominent examples in this regard are the UK Modern Slavery Act (2015), the Australian Modern Slavery Act (2018), the California Transparency in Supply Chains Act (2012), and the EU Non-Financial Reporting (NFR) Directive (2014/95/EU).[9] The French Due Diligence of Corporations and Main Contractors Law

---

9   The NFR Directive applies to companies that have more than 500 employees and are of significant public relevance because of the nature of their business, size or corporate status, including listed companies, banks, insurance companies and other companies designated by national authorities as public-interest entities. There are an estimated 6,000 in total in the EU. They are required to report on how the company's performance, position and activities affect environmental, social, employee, human rights, anti-corruption and bribery issues. Information should cover the company's policies on each issue and their outcomes, its due diligence processes, principal risks, the business relationships, products and services that are likely to cause adverse impacts in those areas of risk, and a description of how the company manages the principal risks (Alliance for Corporate Transparency Project, 2019).

(Devoir de vigilance des sociétés mères et des entreprises donneuses d'ordre) of 2017 goes even further.[10] The law, which applies to companies with more than 5,000 employees in France or 10,000 worldwide (an estimated 150–200 companies), requires that corporations must exercise due diligence in seeking to identify and avoid human rights violations, breaches of fundamental freedoms, violations of health and safety rights and environmental damage. Building on the UN Guiding Principles on Business and Human Rights, this includes the identification of risks, procedures for regular assessments of subsidiaries, subcontractors and suppliers, actions to mitigate risks or prevent serious harm, and mechanisms for alerts and monitoring. Furthermore, the companies must implement a diligence plan setting out these risks and procedures and publish annual reports on progress. The French law, therefore, makes a due diligence approach compulsory and adds the requirement to publish a plan to mitigate risks or prevent serious harm, including mechanism for alerts and monitoring (Brack, 2019: 45–46).

The proposed penalties for failing to prepare such a plan – fines of up to €10 million, or up to €30 million if the failure to develop a plan led to injuries that could otherwise have been prevented – were struck down as unconstitutional in March 2017. The general due diligence obligation and the requirement to implement a diligence plan remain, however, as do civil liability mechanisms in case of failure to implement the plan or if there are weaknesses in it. The state plays no role in compliance; the civil liability mechanisms must be pursued by third parties such as NGOs (Brack, 2019: 45).

While there has undoubtedly been a significant increase in regulatory processes and commitments to due diligence, a key dilemma of many of the above-mentioned initiatives is that they are limited without accountability, transparency and equitable enforcement (Fountain and Huetz-Adams, 2020b: 7).

The European Commission is preparing a draft law on due diligence, which would make EU companies legally responsible for ensuring that their supply chains are sustainable and free of human rights abuses. The Commission plans to present the law in the course of 2021 and recently launched a public consultation, which was open for input from organizations and individuals until February

---

10 The French Devoir de Vigilance law echoes the logic of the OECD's Due Diligence Guidance for Responsible Business Conduct and the UN Guiding Principles on Business and Human Rights, agreed in 2011, which provide guidance on how Parties should operationalize this 'protect, respect and remedy' framework.

2021.[11] Many policymakers and representatives from businesses and civil society have welcomed the initiative, but have also raised questions about what form the new rules might take (i.e. regulation, which is binding EU wide, or directive, which sets the goals and framework, but leaves implementation to EU member countries), as well as the scope of application of the rules.[12]

The EU Parliament's Trade Committee already gave it's blessing to the EU Commission plan for mandatory due diligence laws on deterring deforestation and human rights violations. The Trade Committee approved several far-reaching amendments to the Commission draft, including a requirement that companies respect core labour standards and environmental commitments throughout the entire supply chain, rather than only from their immediate 'tier one' suppliers. Conservative MEPs had previously pushed back against the measure, arguing that in supply chains with several layers of production, such as for clothes and shoes, it was impossible to keep tabs on all the suppliers contributing to a single product. Committee members also argued that 'new EU legislation should further include robust enforcement mechanism and access to grievance mechanisms in Europe to victims,' and called for 'complementary measures', including a ban on imports of products linked to 'severe human rights violations' such as forced or child labour.[13]

There are also initiatives within the UN System to develop instruments for implementing the UN Protect, Respect and Remedy Framework.[14] The Human Rights Council adopted the Guiding Principles on Business and Human Rights in June 2011. In June 2014, the UN Human Rights Council established an Intergovernmental Working Group tasked with the elaboration of an international legally-binding instrument to regulate, in international human-rights

---

11 See: https://ec.europa.eu/info/law/better-regulation/have-your-say/initiatives/12548-Sustainable-corporate-governance/public-consultation?utm_source=POLITICO.EU&utm_campaign=f916e5b529-EMAIL_CAMPAIGN_2020_10_28_05_59&utm_medium=email&utm_term=0_10959edeb5-f916e5b529-189810753

12 For more detail, see: www.politico.eu/event/csr-for-supply-chains/?utm_source=POLITICO.EU&utm_ campaign=f916e5b529EMAIL_CAMPAIGN_2020_10_28_05_59&utm_medium=email&utm_term=0_10959edeb5-f916e5b529-189810753

13 For more information, see: Politico Morning Trade Europe, 28 October 2020.

14 The UN Human Rights Council endorsed this framework in 2008. For more detail, see: https://media.business-humanrights.org/media/documents/files/reports-and-materials/Ruggie-protect-respect-remedy-framework.pdf

law, the activities of transnational corporations and other business enterprises – the UN Treaty on Business and Human Rights. Till the end of 2020 there have been six rounds of negotiations on this draft Treaty (for more information see Burrow, 2019). Negotiating progress is however slow, as many Western nations – including member states of the European Union and forces within the European Commission – continue to block significant measures, with the EU not even participating in the negotiations (Fountain and Huetz-Adams, 2020b: 15).

Most of the large agro-food processing, trading and retail companies already report significant amounts of information on due diligence, but this has not succeeded in resolving the key problems. Although a legislative reporting requirement could help to standardize the information collected, and create a level playing field for company reporting, it seems unlikely that on its own and in a stand-alone function it would result in transformational change in the sector (Brack, 2019: 40). It can however give NGOs and producer groups and associations a potentially powerful tool to disclose precarious practices and conditions and initiate countervailing legal action (such as in cases of unlawful eviction of farmers from their land, inhuman employment of migrant workers, illegal clearing of tropical forests or commercial use of protected areas).

With the 'investor-state dispute settlement' (ISDS) companies have a powerful legal instrument to challenge government policy. ISDS is a system through which investors can sue countries for discriminatory practices. ISDS can be found in public international law, and in a number of bilateral investment treaties and in certain international trade treaties. Conversely, communities, groups or individuals have not yet any legal instrument under which they can charge companies with headquarters abroad for violations of human rights and environmental damage. Due diligence legislation would therefore level the 'legal playing field'. As Fountain and Huetz-Adams (2020b: 8) correctly emphasize:

Current forms of certification and farm-based standards increase pressure on farmers: instead, we need laws that hold the powerful accountable, rather than laws which demand that farmers change. Compliance criteria are imbalanced and need restructuring so that companies are held accountable to due diligence systems.

B. International Coordination and Supply Management

As important as it is for farmers, rebalancing power in international supply chains can on its own not overcome one principal problem plaguing international agri-food markets: potential oversupply and the resulting depression and volatility of commodity prices. In particular productivity boosts have increased the propensity to oversupply and VSS-compliant production has not insignificantly contributed to that trend: improving quality and productivity of produce have not only been an integral part of many VSS schemes; productivity boosts have been imperative to cover or overcompensate VSS compliance costs. In other words, to assure that farmers get appropriate living incomes or salaries in the end will require some form of international coordination and supply management that avoids that any additional revenue derived from a strengthened bargaining position at national level and productivity increases is not jeopardized by depressed or volatile international commodity prices. As said before, without socio-economic sustainability the achievement of environmental sustainability remains illusory: the two poles have to be thought of and conceptualized in tandem.

What we deal with here is a situation of a single product group or food commodity item (coffee, cocoa, tea, bananas, pineapples, a cereal, cotton, wood etc.) that is produced, refined, manufactured, transported and sold within an international supply chain.

To start with, any international coordination of supply must be built on the shoulders of an effective national coordination of production, be it through state or government-supported institutions, like marketing boards or well-organized and strong producer associations.

Ever since the demise of International Commodity Agreements (ICAs), one of the most polarized debates on commodity issues has been that of supply management at international level. As Green (2005: 24) correctly points out,

> the debate resembles little more than a dispirited counsel of despair. Resigned to falling prices and increasing marginalization, policy makers and opinion formers can only advocate aid, managed decline (e.g. by smoothing prices) and exit for an increasingly trapped residual group of poor countries that have so far failed to find the way out of commodity dependence. Yet donors have few ideas, confining themselves to repudiating past remedies and stressing the need for an 'enabling environment' for private sector investment.

ICAs, operational for several commodities in the 1970s and 1980s, offer plenty of insight and lessons on what institutional forms and functional mechanisms worked more or less well. The key problems that ICAs faced were (i) to limit production at a time when productivity increases were expanding supply; (ii) lack of enforcement mechanisms regarding production and export quotas; (iii) the difficulty to anticipate future price trends and to agree on appropriate price ranges; (iv) the free-rider problem (i.e. that some producing countries remained outside the ICAs or new producers emerged outside the agreement); and (v) the impact of developed country agricultural policies and related subsidies in undermining the agreement for products also produced in the North, such as cotton.

Whatever their flaws might have been, undoubtedly there were several successful ICAs. Besides OPEC, the best known and most discussed ICA is that for coffee, which lasted from 1975–1989. The Agreement regulated exports and imports within price bands, but the economic clause in the agreement was abandoned in 1989 (mostly for ideological reasons in the nascent era of deregulation and liberalization). Until that moment, governments in both producing and consuming countries sought to agree to pre-determined supply levels by setting export quotas for producing countries. The aim was to keep the price of coffee relatively high and stable, within a price band ranging from US$1.20–US$1.40 per pound. The agreement succeeded in stabilizing prices and persistently raised them by 24–30 percent over what would otherwise have been market clearing levels. In the six years following the collapse of the ICA for coffee, international prices fell between 60 and 65 percent (Green, 2005: 36).

One conceivable option for international supply management[15] that could also incorporate specific environmental objectives is the concept of international commodity-related environment agreements (ICREAs), a possible instrument for correcting international commodity underpricing.

1. The Concept of International Commodity-Related Environment Agreements

New commodity pricing arrangements that reflect the costs and benefits of environmental protection are essential to promoting sustainable development.

---

15 Article XX (h, i and j) of GATT 1947 has a limited exception for international commodity agreements. In various free trade agreements, such as the EU FTAs with African countries, this exception has been purposefully deleted. For a more elaborate analysis, see Lunenborg (2009).

Through negotiated cost prices, ICREAs could internalize part of the costs associated with the introduction of clean technologies, commodity diversification, and sustainable management practices (including social issues). The costs are then borne by the beneficiaries of the services rendered by the commodities. Revenues could be managed by the administrative body of the ICREA. These agreements would conceptually have two windows of operation:

- A first window would deal with international supply management to avoid depressed price levels and high price volatility. This would safeguard an international price level that assures an appropriate living income for farmers and farm workers. It could be achieved through a mechanism of production and export quotas among producing countries and a coordination of investment plans.
- A second window, run in parallel, would deal with commodity-specific social and environmental issues in relation to international trade. The underlying objectives in this regard are:
  - Internalize environmental and social externalities in the price of exported commodities so that the ultimate consumers in the long term pay a large part of the true resource and social costs;
  - Promote eco-friendly and socially sustainable production methods for a specific primary export commodity;
  - Support governments of exporting countries in developing supportive ecological and social policies for the export sector;
  - Contribute to the diversification of production and export in those developing countries where natural preconditions are not fit for producing the commodity in an environmentally and socially sound way, but where a lack of alternative foreign exchange sources would otherwise impede participation.

ICREAs – developed as a concept and policy discussion proposal in the early 1990s by Dutch economist Henk Kox and one of the authors of this book working at UNCTAD at that time (see Kox, 1993) – aim at helping commodity exporting countries to implement more sustainable production methods either through eliminating the competitiveness impacts of environmental policies providing revenue for improving production methods or guaranteeing a price premium for more sustainably produced commodities. Although the original concept did not include the function of international coordination and supply management,[16] this appears indispensable if one wants to avoid the risk of oversupply, jeopardizing all socio-economic objectives on assuring sufficient living income or wages for producers. For ICREAs to work, they need to be (i) sector-specific; (ii) multilaterally agreed between producing and consuming countries[17]; (iii) implemented with full government support; and (iv) exempt from challenge in the WTO.[18]

Depending on the market and production conditions for the commodity, the second window of an ICREA may take several forms, all of which are intended to promote the use of technologies for sustainable production. Whatever the form, however, socio-economic effectiveness of the agreement would significantly depend on international supply management that needs to be part of the ICREA as the first window. The second window could conceptually be shaped in four ways:

Transfer ICREA	International compensation fund for commodity-specific environmental projects and programmes. Fund contributions are contractually agreed and proportional to imports.
Policy synchronization ICREA	Synchronized introduction of environmental standards or other environmental policies with regard to the particular export sector.
Voluntary fund ICREA	International compensation fund for national commodity-related environmental projects and programmes. Contributions to the fund are voluntary and not proportional to imports.
Eco-label ICREA	Issuing and certification of commodity-specific eco-label(s) to create a market premium for sustainably produced commodities.

---

16 This was primarily not for conceptual, but political reasons given reigning neoliberalism at the time.

17 Although the conclusion of multilateral agreements has been rare in recent years because of the crisis of multilateralism, some international environmental agreements have been negotiated.

18 The GATT 1947, Article XX (h, i and j) allowed commodity agreements in some circumstances.

With the benefit of hindsight, the most promising type for the second window of ICREAs seems to be the eco-label one, based however on a state-determined basic framework (a sort of public standard on social and ecological requirements) supplemented by VSS schemes that go beyond those floor requirements and therefore might fetch a price premium on product qualities or production processes, without however undercutting supply management settings in window one.

In 1995, the UNCTAD secretariat presented an analytical document to the Standing Committee on Commodities of the UNCTAD Trade and Development Board, entitled Sustainable Development and the Possibilities for the Reflection of Environmental Costs in Prices that included ICREAs as a conceivable institutional mechanism (UNCTAD, 1995). While the suggestion got a cold shoulder from the US and a lukewarm reaction from the EU (asking for more research on the subject), the initiative had broad support from the developing world, especially Asian countries. In the light of the feet-dragging of Northern countries, UNCTAD launched operational activities in interested South-East Asian countries to discuss the issue of cost internalization for natural rubber exports in the context of informal commodity roundtables, proposed as a fallback option in case of disagreement on ICREAs. Several of these roundtables were held with the support of UNCTAD as part of the recurrent International Rubber Forum, organized by the International Rubber Study Group in the late 1990s and early 2000s.

C. Lifting the Bar of Sustainability Performance: How Can VSS Play a Constructive Role in the Future?

As Glasbergen (2018: 248–250) correctly criticizes,

> the world of private conditions for modern agricultural production of commodities has become too much an end-in-itself: a market of competing governance mechanisms, focused on marketing partial change, influencing access to market of only small groups, and probably with a temporary effect. What is at stake here is the legitimacy of the whole system of private sustainability claims ... Answers to improve the system of standards and certification are generally sought within the narrow confines of the standards and certification schemes of a specific

crop. This results in an important but a restricted collection of improvement of the legitimacy of the existing arrangements, such as a focus on transparency, accountability, representation, and the necessity to better monitor and evaluate the arrangements, which is comparable to suggesting a catalyst or airbag in a car. They contribute to safer and cleaner driving (social and environmental benefits), which are important changes, but it is still a car and driving it remains a risky and polluting activity. By investing in optimizing the safety and eco-friendliness of a car, one may neglect other solutions that may lead to more systemic changes, e.g. the transition from private car use to public transport.

Against this background and on the shoulders of publically set sustainability requirements, VSS could supplement public sustainability objectives and go 'an extra mile' to lift the bar of sustainability performance in respect of specific objectives or in a cross-cutting way.

1. Is the Constructive Use of VSS in the European Union's Generalised Scheme of Preference (GSP) an Option?

The EU's GSP is a preferential trade arrangement by which the EU grants unilateral, non-reciprocal preferential market access to goods produced in developing countries, pursuant to a 1979 decision by the Contracting Parties to GATT 1947, known as the so-called 'Enabling Clause' (GATT, 1979). The most recent version of the EU's GSP scheme (EU Regulation No. 978/2012) consists of three arrangements: (i) the 'Standard GSP'; (ii) the special incentive arrangement for sustainable development and good governance, also termed 'GSP+'; and (iii) the special arrangement for the least-developed countries (LDCs), also known as 'Everything but Arms' (EBA). Box 7 summarizes the key features of the three clusters of the EU's GSP scheme as well as the resulting tariff preferences.

Box 7: The key features of the EU's GSP scheme and the applicable tariff preferences[19]

The three GSP clusters and their features

Standard GSP	Special rules on sustainable development and good governance (GSP+)	Special rules for LDCs (EBA)
– Rules apply to countries that have not been classified by the World Bank as 'high' or 'upper-middle-income country' for 3 consecutive years. – Rules apply to countries that do not take advantage of any other equally beneficial special rules (e.g. bilateral trade agreements). – Tariffs for 'non-sensitive goods' (i.e. that do not have an impact on EU producers) are completely removed. – Tariffs for 'sensitive goods' (i.e. that do have an impact on EU producers) are reduced by 3.5–20 percentage points.	– Rules apply to countries, whose export of the 7 biggest GSP product groups to the EU account for more than 75 percent of total exports, and whose exports to the EU do not account for more than 2 percent of total EU imports. – Ratification of 27 international conventions on core human and labour rights as well as on environment and governance issues with a commitment to implementation.	– Rules apply to LDCs only, as classified by the UN. – Tariffs removed for all goods except arms and ammunition. – Import licenses required for certain products, such as sugar cane.
– Product graduation rules (relevant for the discussion as exports from larger commodity exports would be outside the scope of GSP and thus the issue of promoting VSS in the context of GSP would be moot – however it seems that GSP+ does not have the same product graduation criteria) – Exclusions – also reduce the utility of GSP to promote VSS	– A regular monitoring mechanism checks implementation. – Tariff preferences to be suspended if the country breaches the international conventions it has ratified.	

---

19 This box draws on information in the study of Marx et al. (2018).

Summary of tariffs applied under the three different GSP clusters

Type of product	Approximate share of EU tariff lines	Examples	Standard GSP	GSP+	EBA
Not sensitive	26%	Pistachios, grapefruit, sun-cured oriental type tobacco, aircraft, ships, headgear, articles of iron and steel	Free (exceptions for agricultural products with non-ad valorem rates)	Free (exceptions for agricultural products with non-ad valorem rates)	Free
Sensitive	40%	Potatoes, pineapples, avocados, fish, spirits (except rum), clothing, shoes, vehicles	Reduced duty (usually 3.5 percentage points; 20 percent reduction for clothing)	Free (exceptions for agricultural products with non-ad valorem rates)	Free
Excluded from GSP/ GSP+ and MFN rate > zero	9%	Beef, pork, poultry, bananas, sugar, wine, rum	No preference, MFN rate applies	No preference, MFN rate applies	Free (excluding arms and ammunition of chapter 93)
MFN zero	25%	Raw coffee beans, cocoa beans, crude oil, pharmaceuticals, gold, most IT products	Free	Free	Free

Conceptually VSS could be used under the EU's GSP scheme to link trade preferences to compliance with specifically relevant VSS. However, this is easier said than done because under prevailing GSP conditions there are only very few product groups and developing countries for which VSS compliance would actually result in additional tariff preferences. Generally, the share of EU imports from developing countries under the GSP scheme is very low and has declined even further in recent years (from some 6 percent in 2011 to 4 percent in 2016), whereas imports under zero tariffs remained very high (between 70–75 percent) and the share of imports under free trade agreements soared from 10 to 13 percent. Under GSP+, some 98 percent of imports and under EBA virtually 100 percent are duty-free. Under the Standard GSP cluster, tariffs still play some role for fisheries, fresh edible fruit and nuts, apparel and textiles as well as footwear, yet one of the most important apparel and footwear exporting countries to the EU – Bangladesh – falls as LDC under the zero-tariff treatment of the EBA cluster. What is more, additional costs for VSS implementation and conformity assessment might not even out the tariff benefits arising from the GSP scheme, in particular when certain countries might benefit from other preferential trade treatment options (Marx et al., 2018: 40, 41, 52).[20]

Another argument often advanced is reduced GSP implementation cost because through VSS use GSP enforcement would be 'outsourced' and the EU would have the ability to govern 'beyond EU borders' (Marx et al., 2018: 37). What should however not be overlooked is the fact that the EU's GSP is a state to state scheme, in which VSS can at best play some complementary role along the lines outlined below.

From a conceptual point of view, VSS could also be integrated into authorized Economic Operator Schemes where certain exporters could benefit from trade facilitative measures if they comply with certain standards.[21] The incentive would then not be tariff concessions, but trade facilitation (e.g. fewer inspections, simplified documentation etc.).

---

20 It should not be overlooked that giving preferential treatment to certified goods will inevitably call for even stricter controls and procedures. In addition, it risks to even more accentuate that it will be the standards of the importing country that should apply. This might make VSS caught in the same discussions as other TBT issues.

21 An Authorized Economic Operator (AEO) is defined by the World Customs Organization's SAFE Framework of Standards as a party involved in the international movement of goods, in whatever function, that has been approved by, or on behalf of, a national Customs administration as complying with WCO or equivalent supply chain security standards. For more information, see: http://tfig.unece.org/contents/authorized-economic-operators.htm

Theoretically, there is also some room for deploying VSS in the context of the new European Green New Deal and related EU discussions on applying carbon border adjustment mechanisms to carbon-intensive imports from countries that are not members of the Paris Agreement on Climate Change or are not fulfilling their obligations under the Agreement. It is however still too early to speculate and elaborate on related pathways and practical options (also see ECOS, 2020 and European Parliament, 2021).

2. The Complementary Role of VSS to Regulation on Key Sustainability Issues

As flagged above, VSS have so far not resulted in transformational change as regards the international agro-food economy and markets. In fact, the more effective government regulation is in correcting disequilibrium in market power, phasing out precarious working conditions, and facilitating internalization of true economic, environmental and social costs in prices, the lesser the need for VSS. The latter should instead focus on going beyond publically set sustainability levels, without however undermining the necessary macro and global market equilibrium.

In the past, this interaction between government regulation and VSS has often misleadingly been termed 'co-regulation' (for an elaborate review, see: OECD, 2002). This term camouflages the fact that regulation is the constituent element in the interaction, setting the basic framework of requirements and, provided there is sufficient political will and appreciation, take measures that correct or dampen the effect of systemic market failures or imperfections. The regulation also sets the framework for VSS for constructive interaction. On the shoulders of regulation, VSS can then perform tasks that 'complement' regulation lifting the bar of social and ecological performance without the risk of pushing VSS-compliant producers into a race to the bottom.

Some examples of such complementarity already exist, which are briefly presented as practical options below.

a. Promoting Organic Agriculture

As already mentioned in Section I.G., historically standards on organic agriculture were developed by farmers in a bottom-up way till the 1980s. To safeguard the integrity of organic agriculture and certification, many countries developed national organic regulations to be able to protect honest organic producers and consumers against misleading organic claims.[22] The first organic regulations were adopted in the US States of Oregon in 1974 and California in 1979. In Europe, France was the first country to adopt an organic regulation in 1985. EU Regulation 2092/91, covering the labelling of organic food, was adopted in 1991. Such legislation has become a de facto 'floor of requirements for organic produce'. Not in all (for example in the US), but in many countries that adopted organic regulation, voluntary standards on organic agriculture exist in parallel with the regulation and tend to supplement or go well beyond the government-set requirements.[23] The differences between these VSS compared to the EU organic regulation, for instance, are particularly large – all of the requirements of private standards are much more stringent or more specific than the EU organic regulation.[24]

Yet, as was pointed out in Section I.G., organic regulation and voluntary organic standards differ in a significant respect. Most organic regulations focus on practising and propagating organic agriculture just as a chemical-free agronomic technique. In other words, regulation largely has a commercial scope for a product free of agrochemicals, food alteration and genetic modification. That approach does not do justice to the original concept of organic. It reduces the idea to a practice by which external agro-chemical inputs are replaced by natural once, just because this simple form of transition is easily auditable.

Conversely, many voluntary organic standards, in particular those developed in a bottom-up way by farmer organizations, go well beyond the organic regulation by also incorporating social and more ecological aspects, such as that farmers must make a living on their land, production methods must maintain biodiversity and reproduce natural resources, as well as take into account that regional conditions require locally adapted solutions, incorporating the traditional knowledge of the farming community. According to this concept, a farmer is not only a producer of agricultural goods, but also a manager of a reproductive

---

22 Protecting consumers and preventing fraud and free-riding by competitors represent a key rationale for public authorities for intervening with standards. This goal is pursued mainly through the protection of trademarks and brands, the banning of fraudulent or misleading claims, or the obligation of private companies to disclose certain information. For more information, see Rousset et al. (2015).

23 Although reliable and comparable statistics on the importance of private standards are not available for many countries, private organic standards appear to be significant in Austria (60 percent of organic farms), Ireland (99 percent), Luxembourg (58 percent), the Netherlands (27 percent), Sweden (79 percent) and Switzerland (95 percent) (Rousset et al., 2015: 16).

24 A comparison of the stringency and specificity of requirements between the EU organic regulation and the voluntary organic standards Demeter, Naturland and Bioland can be found at: http://www.umweltinstitut.org/fileadmin/Mediapool/Downloads/07_FAQ/Lebensmittel/vergleich_richtlinien.pdf

agro-ecological system with its productive resource base that requires steward-ship and respect to the 'limits to growth'.

If one thinks of a 'public-private partnership' in that private organic stan-dards constructively complement the performance requirements of organic regu-lation, one needs to bear this basic qualitative difference in mind.

It is also important not to overlook the problems that might result from supply-related cost pressure, notably under organic regulation. As organic pro-duce is very diverse and heterogenous, mechanism for the coordination of sup-ply for homogenous products, such as some tropical beverages, fruit, vegetables, grain etc. cannot be applied. However, governments might use financial and fis-cal instruments to reward the generation of public goods and services, in partic-ular under voluntary organic standards. These incentive measures can go a long way in countering the cost-treadmill effect of mass production under organic regulation and result in correcting market fundamentals that fail to internalize (at least to some extent) significant environmental costs in prices of conventional agricultural products. In the absence of effective government action to curb mar-ket concentration in wholesale and retail markets, more and more farmers and producer cooperatives practising various forms of agroecology are developing alternative agri-food networks and marketing tracks through the promotion of direct on-farm sales, farmers' markets, box schemes, collective farmers' shops and community-supported agriculture.[25] Yet, as most of such marketing channels have a local or regional focus and are based on a high reputation of producers, they may not necessarily need organic certification for consumer recognition.[26]

Another example that (in the future) may have some similarity with the 'public-private partnership' approach for organic agriculture is the recently launched German initiative on a 'Green Button' label, a sort of publically framed meta-standard for textiles. It was launched in autumn 2019, prompted by the meagre results of the Partnership for Sustainable Textiles that was formed by the German government pursuant to the Rana Plaza disaster in Bangladesh.

25 This implies the emergence of new norms rooted in direct exchange, proximity, transpar-ency, and ethical production and consumption – a shift from a global 'food from nowhere regime' to a 'food from somewhere regime' (for a more elaborate discussion, see Wezel et al., 2016: 139 and Anderson et al., 2015).

26 Some recent developments that support on-line, direct marketing of food products by farm-ers, such as the 'Taobao-villages' created on Alibaba and livestream-marketing on TikTok in China, may however require certification as they are nation-wide schemes.

The Green Button standard sets requirements for both products and companies. Products must comply with 26 social and environmental requirements and companies are required to demonstrate human rights and environmental due diligence according to a set of 20 criteria based on the UN Guiding Principles on Business and Human Rights as well as sector-specific OECD recommendations. In the currently implemented introductory phase that will last over two years, the scheme will apply to two manufacturing stages only, namely 'cut-make-trim' (production) and 'bleaching and dyeing' (wet processes), not fibre production.

For the time being, the Green Button standard, although created and set by the German government, is voluntary in nature and would be verified by third-party private certification bodies. Many NGOs voice criticism on the new standard. According to the Clean Clothes Campaign the criteria are simply too weak to make a difference with regards to sustainability and ensuring that textile workers are employed in fair and safe conditions. For example, the minimum wage laid out in the framework is so low that no one could live off it.[27] Despite its weaknesses and provided there is sufficient political will, the Green Button standard would have the potential to be turned into a compulsory, legally set floor requirement in the future (ideally closely linked to the recently adopted due diligence legislation in Germany for international supply chains), which could then be supplemented by VSS to lift the bar of sustainability performance.

A recent paper on the effectiveness of sustainability standards for cotton production in Africa comes to similar conclusions as regards a constructive interplay between public regulation and VSS. Partzsch et al. (2019) conclude that

> while certification schemes are meant to fill some of the gaps in social and environmental regulation, this form of private governance is largely failing to do so in the case of sustainability concerns in cotton production. Instead, it is possible to argue that some schemes are even 'diluting' (Interview with NGO representative, 3 November 2017) the public standard of the EU Organic Regulation. Bernstein and Cashore (2007) are optimistic about the ability of private governance and voluntary certification systems to regulate markets in the reality of diminished state regulatory capacity. However, according to our empirical findings, this form of governance only appeared as a promising approach in the case of fourth-party certification. A detailed content analysis of the dominant private schemes in Sub-Saharan Africa – Better Cotton Initiative, Cotton made in Africa and FLO – revealed a lack of tenacity in

---

27 Interview of Uwe Wötzel of the Clean Clothes Campaign with the news organization Redaktions- Netzwerk Deutschland.
See: https://www.dw.com/en/germany-unveils-green-button-for-sustainable-textiles/a-50351898

addressing pollution from cotton cultivation inputs. In conclusion, we suggest that NGOs' campaigns should promote public standards and advocate for tightening them up, particularly in the case of EU and USDA Organic, rather than investing their limited resources in participation in multi-stakeholder initiatives. Moreover, with regard to Sub-Saharan Africa, NGOs might promote new bi- and multilateral state agreements; for example, regarding the recognition of public organic standards of producing countries for the EU and US market. Otherwise, if NGOs maintain their commitment to multi-stakeholder initiatives, they risk contributing to 'green-washing' corporate conduct by mobilizing consumer support for labelling programs that actually fall behind existing public regulation on organic certification. Private regulation is only a second-best solution when considering environmental pollution concerns in cotton cultivation supply chains from the perspective of NGOs and their environmental sustainability demands.

b. Using VSS in the Context of Incentive-Based Public Agri-environment Programs

Another example of the complimentary use of food-commodity-related VSS may be their deployment in the context of incentive-based public programs. For instance, agri-environment programs exist in quite a number of developed and also some developing countries. These programs link public financial support to particular ecological performance levels (e.g. in terms of crop diversification, biodiversity conservation, grassland preservation, crop protection strategy, fertilization, nitrogen contamination in soil, climate-change mitigation and adaptation). Regulation could set the floor performance level and VSS could, based on a traffic-light system, go beyond that and thus reward certified farmers with higher public financial support payments. It goes without saying that such public programs would be most effective if they led to or were part of a comprehensive approach towards better reflecting true social and environmental costs as well as environmental benefits in farm production costs. If need be, as seen above for tropical beverages or below for the case of dairy farmers, this might also require an endeavour to coordinate supply.

Such an approach seems more suited to programmatic policies that involve a host of criteria, concrete measures and performance results. Conversely, individual agri-environmental measures, such as reduction of pesticides or fertilizer uses or surplus phosphates from manure might also be achieved by resorting to environmental taxes or charges on pesticides (like in Denmark, France, Italy, Norway and Sweden), taxes on applied fertilizers (such as in Italy)[28] or tradable permits on surplus phosphates from manure (as in the Netherlands) (for more information see Rousset et al., 2015: 24–25).

c. Reforming the Dairy Market

Another example of a regulatory approach, complemented by VSS is currently under discussion for reforming milk production and the dairy sector in the European Union. The EU discontinued its quota-based supply management system of milk in 2015. Ever since, however, milk prices have been very volatile and fell to such a depressed level in recent years that farm-gate prices were well below production costs. The recent decision to address the milk oversupply crisis with the activation of private storage aid did however not get a warm welcome from most dairy farmers. The European Milk Board, for instance, said in early May 2020 that while the EU market was flooded with milk (oversupply was in the order of 15–20 percent) and prices were in a downward spiral, only EU-wide coordinated production cuts could bring about market relief.[29]

If a milk supply coordination scheme were reactivated at the EU-wide level[30] and public corrective measures were also taken through competition policy to limit the disproportionate market power of large dairy companies and supermarkets so that critically important market fundamentals were corrected, VSS could be deployed to obtain price premiums for generating particular environmental and social goods and services. This could, for instance, apply to pasture or organic milk or other forms of extensive milk-cow management, distinct from factory-like production, based on high-performance dairy cattle breeds mostly using imported protein-rich feed.

28 The efficiency of related taxes or levies on problematic agro-chemical inputs is a controversial issue, because to have a noticeable effect would require very high tax rates (see Buntzel, 1992).
29 See: www.dairyreporter.com/Article/2020/05/05/Events-planned-as-EMB-ramps-up-opposition-to-storage-aid?utm_source=newsletter_daily&utm_medium=email&utm_campaign=05-May-2020
30 According to ZMB Dairy World, till 2015, almost 30 percent of global cow milk supply was subject to government-set supply-quota controls. With the complete liberalization of the EU milk market in 2015, supply management arrangements only covered 3 percent of world milk supply, largely confined to Canada, Norway, Japan and Israel.

d. The Role of VSS in Implementing the EU Renewable Energy Directive

The EU Renewable Energy Directive (RED) was adopted in 2009 and set a number of mandatory targets to promote the use of renewable energy, including biofuels. RED defined a number of social and environmental sustainability criteria that domestically and imported biofuels should fulfil. The application of certain VSS was singled out as 'proof of compliance' with the sustainability criteria in RED.[31] Since July 2011, the EU has recognized a total of 19 VSS, some of which are privately run, including developed by NGOs in so-called roundtable consortia, others were created by biofuel producers.[32]

As conceptually tempting as this approach might appear, with the benefit of hindsight the way it has been designed and implemented by the EU Commission turned out to be profoundly flawed in terms of substance and procedure. From a substantive point of view, in the last few years, a large number of studies has called in question the effectiveness of an increasing use of biofuels for the replacement of conventional fuel in particular in the transport sector. In fact, virtually all these studies highlight that, when indirect land-use change is taken into consideration, biofuels do more environmental and social harm than good when compared to fossil fuels. A just released study of Environmental Action Germany and Rainforest Foundation Norway, for instance, concludes that enhanced biofuel use can be up to three times more harmful to our climate than conventional fuel consumption.[33] Besides, a number of serious socio-economic problems of

31 One key reason for resorting to this 'proof of compliance' role of VSS is the fact that biofuels, although an agricultural product, are trade-wise not consistently classified as such. For example, ethanol is considered an agricultural product and is therefore subject to the rules under the WTO Agreement on Agriculture, whereas biodiesel is classified as an industrial product and is therefore not subject to the disciplines of the Agreement on Agriculture. Under the environmental window of the latter, WTO Member Countries can define and notify an environmental programme, for which they can apply relatively flexible supportive or corrective measures. This, however, is far more problematic for industrial goods under WTO rules.

32 The RED-recognized 19 VSS shall check that (i) production of biofuel feedstock does not take place on land with high biodiversity; (ii) land with a high amount of carbon has not been converted for biofuel feedstock production; and (iii) biofuel production leads to sufficient greenhouse gas emissions savings. For the list of recognized VSS, see: https://ec.europa.eu/energy/en/topics/renewable-energy/biofuels/voluntary-schemes

33 Environmental Action Germany and Rainforest Foundation Norway (2020). Other recent studies on the subject with similar findings are: Salter et al. (2018) and DeCicco et al. (2016).

increased biofuel production (notably land tenure conflicts, forced/child labour and precarious working conditions) are also not duly taken into account.[34]

From a procedural perspective, an evaluation of the certification of sustainable biofuels under RED by the European Court of Auditors (2016) flagged the following weaknesses: (i) some recognized VSS were found to be insufficiently transparent and suffered from imbalanced governance structures, which could generate conflicts of interest; (ii) once a VSS has been officially recognized, the EU Commission does not check whether the VSS actually applies the certification standards it committed to in its request for recognition; and (iii) the current system does not provide a specific and separate complaints mechanism that renders it vulnerable to violations (for more information see Marx et al., 2018: 29–31).

Although the results of the above-outlined approach have turned out to be highly questionable, the concept as such remains valid, provided there is a clear division of responsibility, a prevailing primacy of regulation and no ambivalent arrangements on 'co-regulation' or 'public recognition of proof of conformity through VSS'.

e. The Complementary Role of VSS to the EU's Forest Law Enforcement Governance and Trade Program

Apart from VSS that deal with cross-cutting social, economic and ecological issues for a particular or several food commodities (e.g. coffee, cocoa, tea, bananas, specific vegetables or milk), there are also cases, in which single issue-focused VSS might be constructively applied in the future. One example in this regard is the EU Forest Law Enforcement Governance and Trade (FLEGT) Voluntary Partnership Agreements (VPAs).

An approach following the ICREA second window logic can be found in the EU's FLEGT Voluntary Partnership Agreements concluded with several timber producing and exporting developing countries in recent years.

FLEGT VPAs have been developed to phase out illegal timber harvesting and international trade from the EU market and supporting forest governance reforms in timber-producing countries. Under the terms of the FLEGT, each partner country must establish a timber legality assurance system (a national traceability system) and an export licensing system to ensure that only timber

---

34 Against this very background, the European Parliament voted to remove biodiesel made from palm oil from the list of biofuels that can count towards the renewables target in 2021.

products that have been produced legally can be licensed for export to the EU (for further detail see Box 8).[35]

Box 8: The EU's Forest Law Enforcement Governance and Trade Program (FLEGT)

A key element of the FLEGT Action Plan is a scheme to ensure that only legally harvested timber is imported into the EU from countries agreeing to take part in this scheme. The internal EU legal framework for this scheme is the FLEGT Regulation adopted in December 2005, and a 2008 Implementing Regulation, allowing for the control of the entry of timber to the EU from countries entering into bilateral FLEGT Voluntary Partnership Agreements (VPAs) with the EU. Once agreed, the VPAs include commitments and action from both parties to halt trade in illegal timber, notably with a license scheme in the partner country and the issuance of FLEGT licenses that certify the legality of timber exported to the EU. To issue FLEGT licenses, a VPA partner country must implement a timber legality assurance system (TLAS) and other measures specified in the VPA.

When fully operational a TLAS is both robust and credible, as it includes adequate supply chain controls, mechanisms for verifying compliance and is subject to independent audits. A VPA TLAS is built around a practical definition of legality that has been agreed through participatory processes involving stakeholders from government, the private sector and civil society. The VPA also promotes better enforcement of forest law and an inclusive approach involving civil society and the private sector. The first VPA was signed with Ghana, followed by the Republic of Congo, Cameroon, Indonesia, the Central African Republic, Liberia and Vietnam. The EU has concluded negotiations and initialled the VPA with Honduras and Guyana. Negotiations are ongoing with Côte d'Ivoire, Democratic Republic of the Congo, Gabon, Laos, Malaysia, and Thailand (European Commission, 2020).

In general, developing legality assurance systems (including national traceability schemes) have been more complex and difficult to establish than initially expected. However, despite the time-consuming process, in many cases the development of the FLEGT VPAs has led to significant improvements in forest governance. In most cases, the VPA negotiations have seen the adoption

---

35   For more information on EU FLEGT VPAs, see: Overdevest and Zeitlin (2016): 60–61 and Marx et al. (2018): 28–29.

of multi-stakeholder processes to agree operational definitions of 'legal timber' and all the agreements contain commitments to regulatory and policy reform to make forest laws clearer and more comprehensive, together with improvements in transparency and stakeholder involvement. The EU and Member States have provided capacity-building assistance to partner countries to help them set up the licensing scheme, improve enforcement and, where necessary, reform laws (Brack, 2019: 28–29).

A study on the FLEGT VPAs progress in Ghana and Indonesia (Overdevest and Zeitlin, 2016: 60–61) concluded that

> the implementation process has led in both countries to substantially increased participation by civil society and other stakeholders in forest governance, greater transparency and accountability of forestry administration, and heightened recognition of community rights. In both countries, too, the VPA process has focused attention on protecting the needs and livelihoods of small producers in the transition to the new timer legality regime . . . the VPA process contributed to reducing arbitrary administrative discretion in forest governance, including the award of concessions and harvesting permits, while creating new mechanisms for exposing corruption across the supply chain, whose effectiveness can be expected to grow as the monitoring, reporting, and review provisions of their timber legality assurance schemes kick into full gear with the onset of FLEGT licensing.

Interestingly, the Civil Society Cocoa Platform in Ghana, which rallies NGOs and community organizations working on cocoa and forests, called for a system similar to the VPAs and the EU Timber Regulation to be applied to cocoa in their submission to the European Commission's consultation on a deforestation action plan. The details of what such system could look like for cocoa were described by Ghanaian and European NGOs in a briefing paper, published in 2018 (see Tropenbos, EcoCare Ghana, Forest Watch Ghana and Fern, 2018).

The most important timber-focused VSS schemes, FSC and PEFC (Programme for the Endorsement of Forest Certification) have taken the legality, tracing and due diligence requirements across the supply chain / chain-of-custody (applying to non FLEGT VPA countries) into due account in recent years. However, in practice it has been observed that VSS certification alone does not suffice to prove legality. This said, however, such VSS can help generate additional environmental and social benefits for forest communities, employees, as well as forests, protected areas and habitats.

While such VSS can play a constructive role to supplement legislation and facilitate more sustainable trade, the key systemic driving forces of illegal logging and shipment, most of them related to economic reasons and rent-seeking activities, must be discussed and dealt with in the course of the bilateral governmental discussions and consultations and then corrected. If that is not the case, VSS schemes for implementing the FLEGT VPAs are fighting a sort of uphill battle.

To the above-mentioned examples one could add a few others, but the image depicted above remains mostly the same. VSS can only play some constructive supplementary role for achieving true sustainability if the principal systemic market failures and distortions are corrected or at least smoothened by governmental intervention. In this regard, the improvement of economic sustainability of a solid body of farmers and not only a few plays a pivotal role.

Before concluding, it should also not go without comment that in the era of enhanced digitalization one may also look at options beyond certification.

> Companies can drive change by becoming more transparent – both about who they are buying from and how the different actors in their supply chain perform. One interesting example is the Chinese Institute of Public and Environmental Affairs' (IPE) Blue Map database, through which companies can track the real-time environmental performance of their Chinese suppliers – including any violations and how these are being resolved. Many Western fashion brands already use this system and some (including Inditex, Gap, Esprit and Puma) supply data to IPE's Green Supply Chain Map, which publicly links them to their suppliers and provides real-time factory-level environmental performance data (IPE, 2018). High levels of transparency and traceability would raise the stakes for consumer-facing companies in Western markets, as they would be publicly accountable for what happens in their supply chains. (Changing Markets Foundation, 2018: 90)

D. Epidemics and VSS: A Relationship that Is None

Nobody else than the famous ingenious philosopher and sociologist, Michel Foucault, used the example of pandemics to decode the epochs of governmentality, analysing the way in which states in European history have reacted to three basic diseases: leprosy in the Medieval times, the pestilence in the times of absolutism, and the smallpox in modern times. While leprosy was fought by the supreme authorities at their times by excluding the sick from society, pestilence later on in history was contained by locking down and isolating the affected communities with total disciplinary power, and to smallpox governments reacted by 'rational self-control' (Foucault, 2004). In our present liberal times the individuals count, the disciplinary power is internalized, thus external power is apparently not needed. Modernity finds its expression in vaccination campaign as answer to epidemics (for instances against smallpox), according to Foucault the breakthrough to civilization. The role of the state is reduced to introduce benchmarks for safety and related rules, surveillances, to collect data, to contain the endemic and to coordinate research. It is assumed that the subjects of society and economy organize themselves along the path the state has marked, to analyse and manage the risks by self-regulating networks (Sarasin, 2020).

It is amazing how precise this type of governance as a reaction to pandemic challenges was predicted and described by Foucault already 45 years ago, long before the Corona crisis. Neoliberal thinking follows this pattern of how to exercise power. To better understand it, Foucault used such apparently inconspicuous phenomena as disease control to explain it. His vision follows pretty much of what we have experienced in the present Corona crisis; similar are also the political approaches to all the other global epidemic threats in recent history, like BSE, MERS, SARS, AIDS, Ebola, Zirka, West Nile Fever, Bird Flu, Swine Fever, Aphthous Fever (Foot and Mouth Disease). That such an outstanding scientific thinker uses biopolicy[36] as a starting point for his theory is visionary, and as a forecast of our present experience with COVID 19 alarming at the same time.

The governance structure of VSS fits perfectly into this liberal scenario, because it matches the ideal of reconstructed pattern of behaviour. The individuals and the private sector take over some responsibility under the guidance of governments to exercise due diligence by installing voluntary mechanism of risk analysis and management, not only for safety reasons, but also as an appendix for the environment, social considerations and economic durability. Governments sit in the driving seat to pilot through the crisis by instruments of incentives and impulses.

The equilibrium between too much and too little governmental interventions is always very precarious in neoliberal settings. Too little can lead to a serious epidemic outbreak, too much may lead to a loss of freedom and personal responsibility. In some cases, however, only strict government-imposed restrictions or bans for individual behaviour guarantee or preserve individual and public freedom in the end. VSS are operating permanently within this dilemma: mandatory or voluntary regulation of sustainability. The fight against an epidemic will

---

36 Later in his academic writing Foucault rejected the term 'biopolicy' to describe the disease containing policy.

tend to swing the pendulum into the direction of more state regulation, at least temporarily.

Times of epidemics are times of the executive, because people are afraid and they ask for action and guidance. Politicians are unable to cope, since they cannot know the character of a new disease or virus. Therefore they get totally dependent upon the advice of their scientific experts. Suddenly technocrats get into the position to co-determine the direction of major political decisions by virtue of their endemic expertise. Technocrats, so far hidden in their laboratories in the basements of clinics and institutes, trying to understand the character of an animalcule, a mutated virus, suddenly rise up to national stars, expected to give advice on something as big as an epidemic, affecting the whole society.

This dimension of a 'Tyranny of Experts'[37] was not factored in Foucault's theory, but is an inherent part of the neoclassical model. The globalized world, placing all the trust on markets, technologies and self-regulating networks, has been turned into something so complicated that the dependency upon experts has become imperative. Pandemic crises expose this trend to its extreme, and disseminate it among many aspects of life, among others also to the world of food and agriculture. While over decades farmers were the stewards of practical sustainability, something very grass rooted, suddenly sustainability becomes the matter of auditors, technocrats and exists only if it is documented, verified and certified by distant standard organizations.

We have to recall: Most of the major VSS came into being around the turn of the century, set in motion by the new food safety laws of the EU in response to the BSE crisis, which hit Europe viciously. According to the new regulations, full liability for the safety of the food they sell was imposed on the European retailers. They had to install a system of traceability for all the items they sell. The consumers might look at labelled food in the way that the environmental aspects are the focus, taking the safety aspects of the food for granted by law. However, for the traders – and thus the VSS – the safety aspect remains crucial. Other criteria of sustainability of food and agriculture are just supplementary, once the basics of the VSS-system are installed. By VSS the big food corporations managed to shift the major burdens of risk to the farmers and primary processors.

Epidemic viruses originate in most cases from wild animals, from where they find – through mutation – their ways into the productive livestock of modern

---

37 See the writings of Easterly (2013), even if he refers in his book more to the role of economists in development economics.

animal keeping (Andersen et al., 2020). This is especially the case for intensively reared livestock that are often genetically similar within a herd or flock and therefore lack the genetic diversity that provides resilience. The emergence of zoonotic diseases is often associated with environmental changes or ecological disturbances, such as agricultural intensification, an extension of human settlement, encroachments into forests and other habitats.[38] The world gets more and more crowded, and there are much more contacts between wildlife, livestock, pets and human beings nowadays. Never before have so many opportunities existed for pathogens to pass from wild and domestic animals through the biophysical environment to affect people, causing zoonotic diseases or zoonosis. Once they infect humans, also transmitting from person to person, in a globalized world economy with intensive migratory movements and more and more uniform consumption patterns, we are faced with a pandemic. The bird flu (or avian influenza) is a typical example of such a trajectory. The Covid 19 virus is a bit different from most of the other zoonosis, since as of early 2021, there has been no proof that it has also been transmitted via food consumption or air in the presence of wild exotic animals.[39] However, estimates suggest that around 60 percent of all infectious diseases in humans are zoonotic (UNEP, 2016: 18).

The experience with a zoonotic like Corona has again revealed the tight interrelationship between wildlife, livestock, environment and humans. It also highlighted that the social and human conditions also matter in terms of contagion, coping capacities, transmission and impact. Many curative and preventative approaches fail, because poor people – living in marginalized conditions – lack the means for adequate hygiene, cannot afford the medicine or are trapped in desperate situations. This especially refers to migrant workers, as in Indian

---

38 In a new book, Malm (2020), echoing the findings of David Quammens (2013), describes how concrete and direct the causes and implications of the climate crisis, notably deforestation, droughts and loss of biodiversity, result in a 'zoonotic spillover'. In the Ethiopian Highland, in Indonesia and in Easter China, spillover effects are already visible. It is expected, for instance, that till 2050 bats that frequently are transmitters of diseases, will lose large parts of their habitats in South-East Asia. The technical infrastructure of the globalized world will then imply that the impact of these developments will be planetary, like the present Corona pandemic.

39 There is no scientific proof of Covid 19 infected food that infected humans. However it is highly unlikely that the many workers in German slaughter houses, who tested positively for Corona, and are in close contact with the meat of the slaughtered animals, have not infected the meat. In fact the official story about the origin of COVID 19 tells us that it originates from the food sold in wet markets in Wuhan, thus deriving from food consumption.

metropolitan areas, in American orchards, in Colombian coffee plantations, in German abattoirs, in Spanish greenhouses, drivers locked up in their truck cabins on European highways, or illegal immigrants in Southern US states. These most affected groups became hotspots of the epidemic and a threat to the health of other citizens. The lesson we have to learn from this is that safe food can only be maintained by also taking due diligence to violations of environmental and human rights in the complete supply chains.

We can now see that the incidence of a pandemic is a matter of a broader sustainability agenda and should affect the VSS debate. However zoonosis have their origin in planetary destructions, while the VSS deal with sustainability only at the microeconomic level. Hardly any of them tackles the supreme deteriorations leading to vicious, highly infectious viruses through mutation, like stopping deforestation,[40] caring for nature conservation, restoring biodiversity, or mitigating climate change. Even if VSS perfectly fit into the neoliberal frame of governance spelt out by Foucault, theoretically as well as empirically their real contribution to fight the basic origins of all the diseases is minor. The transformational change needed is just too significant for the weak instrument VSS. Like how could one expect from VSS to reverse the trend of mass, industrial livestock production (including the extensive use of antibiotics and the thus resulting risk of the emergence and dissemination of multi-resistant bacteria), chemical over-intensification of agricultural husbandry or monoculture cropping? We cannot ask from VSS more than they can possibly give. However the expectations of the society of pro-VSS organizations, which have been systematically nourished, are much bigger.

In reaction to Covid-19, the VSS claim that their mission to help people to cultivate more in harmony with nature is reassured. Environmental measures like stopping deforestation hampers the emergence of infectious diseases. The standard requirements have not been altered. However VSS operations are affected badly through the epidemic by destabilization of partner communities, interrupting global supply chains, restricting crucial activities like audit, training and all

---

40 With the benefit of hindsight, VSS that include obligations or requirements to restrict or stop deforestation or prevent the marketing of illegally cut timber – all measures that would reduce ecological intrusion into natural habitats – have not been very successful in this regard in recent years. This concerns VSS dealing with timber production and harvesting as well as with oil palm and various biofuel feedstock materials (for more information see Slavin, 2018).

kinds of travel related communication. The introduction of personal protective equipment (PPE) is a hindrance to community life and poor people's resources.[41]

VSS can introduce incremental improvements in modern agriculture. Nevertheless, one could argue that through their little corrections modern agriculture becomes even more respectable. Thus VSS create the illusion that they offer some kind of vehicle to greater resilience and sustainability, but – with few exceptions – in reality they make matters worse.[42] The reaction of mainstream agriculture to zoonotic diseases is always the same: To trust thoroughly modern technology, science and sophisticated managerial capacities, intensifying the course of high yielding varieties, specialization and growth. The very same forces that got us into the crisis are employed to get us out again. There is no tendency associated with VSS to reverse that trend.

The rise of zoonosis can hardly be stopped by a therapeutic response to the outbreak of the disease, despite the massive efforts invested by politics into medical treatments and research in vaccines. The only adequate and root-centred response would be a consistent precautionary approach that would result in real systemic change – either there is a universal effort, or there is none. However, the challenge is just too big to be thinkable. At the same time the threats of rising incidents of epidemics are immense.

While VSS working alongside with mainstream agribusiness search for 'artificial' solutions, non-mainstream farming communities and their value chains are getting automatically disdained and blamed for reinforcing the problem. The campaigns against zoonosis are systematically used to curtail the poor people's economy and get rid of it. This happened during the avian influenza, when banning free ranging fowl keeping, damaging the backyard chicken economy of the poor people in developing countries, while praising the factory farming, even though the outbreak of the bird flu was traced to intensive stock rearing in China. Also under the quarantine measures of Corona the first places to be shut down in Latin America were the open street markets. The primary line of thinking is

---

41 Rain Forest Alliance and UTZ among others have introduced certain measures, like partial remote audits, extending current certification and introducing a special policy for supply shortages. See: www.rainforest-alliance.org/business/sustainable-farming/farm-certifica tion/covid-19-message-to-rainforest-alliance-and-utz-certificate-holders-and-certification -bodies/ and also www.globalgap.org/uk_en/media-events/news/articles/Coronavirus-and-GLOBALG.A.P.-Certification-What-You-Need-to-Know/

42 A typical example is the hopeless attempt of VSS to make safer the use of pesticides and other problematic agro-chemicals. They can never win this race, but the fight absorbs most of the energy (see, for instance, Buntzel and Mari, 2016: chapter 23).

always the same: Since zoonosis evolved from nature, all natural systems of production and trade arouse suspicion as being vectors of infection, and the safety measures turn against them (GRAIN, 2020). Since they constitute the very basis for survival of small farmers, cottage processors and petty traders, it is the poor that the war against epidemics turn against. While the rural economy suffers, the posh supermarkets and shopping malls were allowed first to reopen their doors and allowed the well-to-do urban classes to go shopping again. The clean world behind department stores' doors, under roofs and nicely tiled floors pretend to stand for hygienic cleanness and food safety, in spite of the fact that agribusiness is not the answer but one of the key roots of the problem. But this is the world many VSS are associated with.

What effect does an epidemic have in the long run on changing the structures of food systems?[43] If the people got used to trust the agribusiness food in the supermarkets in times of crisis, might they continue to purchase their food there, also when the crisis is over, to the detriment of informal food markets? Will they get used to eating highly processed and well-packed food from the shelves, instead of from street or wet markets? When they are sensitized to a high level of food hygiene and sustainability claims in times of crisis, will they only go for labelled food in future? Long term structural changes might occur from short term disruptions, which might be the most destructive impact for poor peoples' life and small-scale businesses.

Corona taught us one thing: It exposed the excessive enmeshment of our societies in globalization, including the dependence upon global supply chains, the far-going outsourcing of industrial and agricultural production,[44] and massive human migratory movements. The Corona lock-down included barriers to the free movement of people, and cut off manufacturers from imported inputs. Whether this new enlightenment will however really lead to a fundamental change of regulatory, trade and investment liberalization has still to be seen. Some trust in the system of 'hyper globalization' has undoubtedly faded away. VSS, which tried hard to introduce transparency into international trade, cannot restore what has been lost in times of crisis.[45]

---

43 The WHO does not seem to relate pandemics to our food systems or agribusiness.
44 Virtually only driven by productivity and resource efficiency motives, based on cost constellations that externalize true economic, social and environmental costs even more.
45 Based on various recent studies, a new book of Clemens Arvay (from the Austrian Forum on Science and Environment) concludes that some key health risks are closely linked to environmental destruction. The author points out that the Corona Pandemic is largely a consequence

A pandemic and globalization is of a dual character: It intensifies global coordination in the defence attempts, but it also creates fears and interceptions from globalization. The Corona crisis awakened the awareness that a nation should keep a minimum supply of essential medicine production and protective equipment in order to provide protection to its people in case of a crisis. The total liberalization of the markets for pharmaceutical products in the past led to a global relocation of the production and left countries vulnerable from interrupted supply chains from abroad. This lesson will have for sure also an implication for other essential goods, like food or certain strategic resources. In the longer run, this weakening of the neoliberal trade dogma has to have an effect for the global VSS, which are part of the globalized free trade agenda. It will reduce import dependence on food and strengthen domestic food markets.

A pandemic by definition is global. Since the virus travels worldwide if not contained, the fight against it necessarily needs to be a global undertaking. By multiple mechanisms of threat, some kind of global coordination, global advisory services and financial pressure all countries are pushed to join the common global campaign. All countries have to introduce the same or similar risk management tools and safety measure (i.e. a coherent approach), independent from their level of infection, their financial situation and governmental capacities. Little regard is being taken of different aspects, like which level of different precaution is appropriate in a specific location, which exceptions are acceptable, which measures are affordable. Key is the question: Who has the power to define the terms of the global campaign for early detection and control? We see a similar pattern in all cases: The prosperous societies have the definitional power over the global measures, even though most diseases originated in their food systems, their highly globalized economies and lifestyles, all of which spread the virus worldwide. They are the perpetrator, they cause most of the trouble, and then impose the conditions of the common fight on the victim countries, making them losing twice: as victims of the disease and as obedient actors of inappropriate or ill-placed campaigns.

This injustice of the international dimension was very clearly exposed by the BSE-crisis when it was crystal clear that the industrial methods of animal feeding in Europe created the lethal prions (proteinaceous infectious particles) and spread

---

of an environmental scandal and that policy makers and the media report far too one-sided on the Corona crisis and might therefore create more confusion and harm to public debate and understanding as well as effective countervailing strategies (Arvay, 2020).

polluted material all over the world by trade with live animals and contaminated carcass meal. To allow other countries to participate in global trade with cattle or bovine products, they had to introduce complicated and expensive precautionary systems in their cattle related businesses, even if their involvement in international trade was marginal. In the end the products of free-ranging cattle on large estates in South America or by nomads from Sahel, Namibia or Mongolia that never consumed anything else than local roughage had to be treated the same just like the bovine items from the perverted bovine industry in Europe (Segarra and Rawson, 2001; Buntzel-Cano, 2002). This was the newly introduced international standard of precaution, which became mandatory and entered related VSS automatically.

Foucault was right to put the analysis of epidemics into the center of his thoughts. They will gain more and more importance over our societies and life, and to respond to them by voluntary standards has and likely will be ill-conceived.

E. To Sum up

Our analysis has shown that:

- VSS have found their place in the market, but not so much as instruments of consumers' choice for 'green products', but for brand value, product differentiation, management for supply chains and shift of liability from global corporations to primary producers.
- In virtually all agro-food markets, VSS have become a de facto 'license to operate', enshrined in pre-competitive B2B VSS, but also in many B2C VSS.
- VSS are not particularly efficient in dealing with problems that are rooted in fundamental structures of society, the market or the economy. They do normally work well when they are about a straight substitution of a technology, e.g. chlorine-free paper or GMO-free food. Fundamental problems can – and should – be accomplished by mandatory regulation. VSS can then supplement regulatory requirements or even go beyond those.
- VSS are couched within the market-economics logic fostering more production, trade and consumption. Even though some environmental and social VSS requirements dampen undesirable impact of food products and

production, generally VSS are part of the growth paradigm. Yet, true sustainability remains elusive without paying due attention to and incorporating aspects of consumption reduction and sufficiency.

- Rising shares of VSS-compliant produce in the market are not synonymous of increasing true sustainability or triggering systemic, sector-wide changes. VSS and the endeavour to improve the functioning of their standard systems have largely become an end in themselves.

- VSS have undoubtedly created new markets (such as with agro-chemical free food). It must however be doubted that through such schemes VSS can play a leadership role within the concept of a green economy.

- VSS are also tools that may encourage improvements in efficiency, productivity, innovation, product quality and a desirable shift in production and consumption patterns. Yet, most of the related costs and investment for such improvements are shouldered by producers and public donors (either directly or indirectly through NGOs). Moreover, efficiency gains, productivity and quality improvements do not necessarily strengthen the economic sustainability of most producers, because quality price premiums and producer costs suffer from the cost-treadmill effect (i.e. the race to the bottom), on the one hand, and power asymmetries along the supply chain, on the other.

- Without assuring economic and social sustainability of farmers and farm workers, reflected in appropriate living income and wages, producers' interest in using VSS for upgrading environmental sustainability is low. As long as adequate incomes and resources for all stakeholders in the value chain to live in human dignity are not part of the process, the concept of sustainability stays meaningless.

- The market mechanism encourages shifts and outsourcing of production to least-costly locations (i.e. absolute competitive advantage), but also leads to shifts in competitive position to producers that comply with VSS in the least-costly way. This causes cost pressure, encourages specialization and increasing scale of production and underpins the marginalization of small-scale producers and smallholder farmers, all things that often undermine or contradict truly sustainable agriculture. The whole architecture of VSS is very challenging for small-scale farmers. Most VSS do not have the potential to effectively combat rural poverty. The VSS model is confined to some more well-placed and developed enclaves and has not penetrated marginal areas.

- With an increasing number of competing VSS and pressure to boost productivity to keep adaptation, compliance, inspection and certification costs in check, there is an increasing risk of marginalization of less resourceful producers and a race to the bottom to less ambitious VSS.
- Even if there were willingness of developing country governments to provide flanking support, the extent and the costs of it would be extremely high and demanding. The legal, technical and infrastructural capacity-building needs for effective VSS implementation are generally so immense that the budgetary burdens might eat up a considerable part of the public agricultural investments. For developed countries this is a far less onerous problem, and that is part of the unfair competition VSS create in global trade.
- As regards one of the crown jewels of sustainability standards – organic standards -, the internal contradictions of and external pressure on the organic movement have pushed 'organic' more and more into an agribusiness dependency and converts a movement that advocates system change in food and agriculture into a trade mark for individual (free-of-agro-chemical-residues') products. That is pushing organic standards pretty close to other commercial VSS. The original hope that 'organic' might lead to a transformation of the production system in food and agriculture is therefore fading.
- VSS are at a crossroads, but instead of realizing the systemic, deep-rooted nature of the crisis and conceive of much-required reforms most VSS advocates continue to focus their activities on improving the functioning of the VSS standard system, emulating or disseminating best standard-compliance practice and promoting the use of VSS in public procurement.
- Seeking solutions for key sustainability issues only at farm level implies that the core of the problems lies with bad farming. This is an assumption that is as harmful as it is wrong (Fountain and Huetz-Adams, 2020b: 87).

The Way Forward

- Almost all of the current efforts to increase farmer income are based on technical solutions (increased productivity, crop diversification, use of agro-chemicals and new planting material, increased efforts to improve farming techniques). However, the challenges facing many agri-food sectors are often not technical, but deal with power and political economy, such as price formation, the asymmetrical bargaining power of farmers, unbridled market concentration of multinationals, and a lack of transparency and accountability. Tackling political problems with technical solutions will not foster a sustainable agro-food sector, but simply install another form of a business-as-usual scenario.

- To trigger real, transformational change governmental action on correcting some market fundamentals is required. This would include rebalancing power in global agri-food supply chains, including international coordination and supply management, strengthening and changing the focus of competition policy, limiting the use of restrictive business and trading practices, as well as legislation on due diligence for avoiding precarious employment conditions, infringement of human rights, and environmental damage. Regional, South-South and/or international cooperation is required to provide an enabling environment and to give hands and feet to the implementation of these actions.

- Historically the focus of VSS has been on the farming level. It would however be logical for more care and ambition in the development of these standards to also reflect requirements for actors further down the supply chain. If a farmer is required to change most of his/her business practices to be able to sell the product, why shouldn't the same be asked from large multinational corporations in processing, trade and retail (Fountain and Huetz-Adams, 2020b: 35)?

- As the achievement of economic and social sustainability is the lynchpin for the sustainability drive in general, the implementation of sector-wide commitments to living income seems long since overdue. Net farmer income should become a key performance indicator of any sustainability and related certification programme.

- Existing WTO rules and certain provisions in free trade agreements are complicating the implementation of measures to coordinate commodity supply and limit restrictive business or trade practices. Yet, at the same time, international agreements that link environment, trade and investment issues in a constructive way could be a vehicle for a better enabling environment.

- The order in the field of organic food may be the template: a co-determination among state legislation and private labels which go beyond the obligatory benchmark. Having intervened to correct some market fundamentals, governments could set a publically desirable level of ambition on sustainability objectives as a floor level and VSS could complement by 'travelling an extra mile' of sustainability performance. Enough lessons have been learned from 30 years of experiences with this order to avoid some of its systemic weaknesses, like the tendency of governments to take over completely.

List of Acronyms

4C-Association	The Common Code for the Coffee Community
ANSI	American National Standards Institute
AO	Appellation of Origin
AU	African Union
B2B	Business to Business
B2C	Business to Consumers
BSE	Bovine Spongiform Encephalopathy (Mad Cow Disease)
CAC	Codex Alimentarius Commission
CEN	European Committee for Standardization
COSA	Committee on Sustainability Assessment
CSR	Corporate Social Responsibility
EBA	Everything but Arms (by the EU)
EU	European Union
EUI	European University Institute
EurepGAP	Euro-Retailer Produce Working Group on Good Agricultural Practice
FAO	Food and Agricultural Organization of the United Nations
FiBL	Forschungsinstitut für biologischen Landbau [Research Institute on Organic Agriculture, located in Switzerland]
FLEGT	EU Forest Law Enforcement Governance and Trade Program
FLO	Fairtrade Labelling Organization International
FNC	Columbian National Coffee Growers Federation

FPEAK	Fresh Produce Exporters Association of Kenya
FSC	Forest Stewardship Council
FTA	Free Trade Agreement
GAP	Good Agricultural Practice
GATS	General Agreement on Trade in Services
GATT	General Agreement on Tariff and Trade
GSP (GSP+)	Generalised System of Preferences (of the EU)
GTZ	German Technical Cooperation Agency
HACCP	Hazard Analysis and Critical Control Points
HCDA	Horticultural Crops Development Agency (in Kenya)
ICA	International Commodity Agreement
ICCO	International Cocoa Organization
ICREA	International Commodity-related Environment Agreement
IEC	International Electrotechnical Commission
IFOAM	International Federation on Organic Agricultural Movements
IIED	International Institute for Environment and Development
IISD	International Institute for Sustainable Development
IMF	International Monetary Fund
INMETRO	National Institute of Metrology, Standardization and Industrial Quality (in Brazil)
IPES-Food	International Panel of Experts on Sustainable Food Systems
ISEAL Alliance	International Social and Environmental Accreditation and Labelling Alliance
ISO	International Standard Organization
ITC	International Trade Center
LCA	Life Cycle Assessment
LDC	Least Developed Country
LMC	LMC International Ltd – consulting firm on agriculture & agribusiness
MRL	Maximum Residue Level
MT	Metric tonnes
NFR	EU Non-Financial Reporting Directive
NGO	Non-Governmental Organization
NOGAMU	National Organic Movement of Uganda
NOP	National Organic Program (of the USDA) in the United States
OECD	Organization for Economic Cooperation and Development
OPEC	Organization of Petroleum Exporting Countries
PDO	Protected Designation of Origin
PEFC	Program for the Endorsement of Forest Certification
PGI	Protected Geographical Indicators

PGS	Participatory Guarantee System
PPP	Public Private Partnership
QR-Code	'Quick response'
RED	Renewable Energy Directive (of the EU)
SABS	South African Bureau of Standards
SDG	Sustainable Development Goals (of the UN)
SIA	Sustainable Impact Assessment
SPS	Sanitary and Phytosanitary (Agreement of the WTO)
TBT	Technical Barrier to Trade (Agreement of the WTO)
TLAS	Timber Legality Assurance System
TSG	Traditional Specialties Guaranteed
UNCED	United Nations Conference on Environment and Development
UNCTAD	United Nations Conference on Trade and Development
UNEP	United Nations Environment Program
UNFSS	United Nations Forum on Sustainability Standards
UNIDO	United Nations Industrial Development Organization
USDA	US Department of Agriculture (Ministry)
UTZ	UTZ-Kapeh; 'good coffee' in the Maya-language
VOCSI	Voluntary Coffee Standard Index
VPA	Voluntary Partnership Agreement
VSS	Voluntary Sustainability Standards
WTO	World Trade Organization
ZMB	Zentrale Milchmarkt Berichterstattung (Diary World Milk Information)

Explanations of Some Technical Terms[1]

accreditation
Official recognition and authorization of persons or institutions that conduct a certification process.

agri-environmental measures (or services)
The EU Common Agricultural Policy pays to farmers a fixed award if they comply with one of the defined environmental measures.

asymmetrical market power
There is a huge difference in matters of size, capital assets and economic importance between the supplier and the buyer in the market, which may lead to unfavourable terms for the inferior party in commercial transactions.

B2B-standard
A standard agreed among different businesses, giving some quality assurance to the buyers, mostly not identified by a label.

B2C-standard
A standard aimed to transmit quality assurance to the end consumers, mostly connected with a label.

certification
A formal procedure to verify conformity with the requirements of a given standard by an accredited institution, leading to a written certificate.

---

1 The explanations given are not necessarily the legal or scientific definitions.

chain of custody	The identity preservation of a special quality of a product over all stages of processing and handling, keeping it separate throughout.
commodity agreement	An international commodity agreement is an undertaking by a group of countries to stabilize supplies and prices of an internationally traded commodity for the benefit of participating countries and producers therein. Such agreements usually reach consensus on traded quantities, prices, and stock management. Some agreements serve solely as forums for information exchange, analysis, and policy dialogue.[2]
conformity assessment	To demonstrate that a product meets all necessary requirements (here of standards).
consumerism	The idea to bring fundamental change to the economy by consumers' choice for goods produced in an environmentally friendly or preferable way.
contract farming	The farm is bound by a contract with the buyer that imposes several conditions on the producer, which might be restrictive.
due diligence	A behaviour of vigilance, attentiveness and care.
epidemic	Outbreak of disease confined to one part of the world
equivalence	Some kind of acknowledgement of one state's technical requirements and conformity assessment system by another state.
ex-/inclusion	Here: Referring to barriers to access certain programs for smallholder producers, because of lack of capacities.
Fairtrade	A set of standards claiming to protect and support the producers' communities in global trade.
food mileage	The distance all inputs of a product have to travel from their place of origin to the place of final consumption.
food sovereignty	A multidimensional concept of food security, which includes the availability of food, access to food, biological utilization of food, and stability. It implies a food system, which is more just.
Global South	Synonymous with the ill-defined meaning of Developing Countries.
Good Agricultural Practice (GAP)	Best managerial or professional practice of how to run a farm.

---

2 See also: https://en.wikipedia.org/wiki/International_commodity_agreement

green economy	An altered economy which stays within the planetary boundaries.
greenwashing	Uncouth term to potentially fake claims, pretending to be environmentally friendly.
harmonization	The highest degree of equivalence
hygiene (of foodstuff)	Food that is safe to consume for human health and nutritious.
informal markets	Markets in Developing Countries, which are hardly regulated, mostly wet or street markets, with little barriers to access.
label	A protected logo tagged to a product guaranteeing a certain quality or special feature to the buyers.
liability	Here: The retailers of food are fully responsible for the safety of the food they sell from field to the shelf.
life-cycle assessment	Attempt to assess the environmental impact of a product from the 'cradle-to-grave'.
living income	To achieve a minimum income necessary for a farmer's family to meet their basic needs by receiving a remunerative price for cash-crops produced.
macro-economic	Relates to the whole national economy.
marketing boards	Para-state enterprises that interfere by legislation into select domestic markets of agricultural commodities with the aim to stabilize prices at a reasonable level (this may include the holding of stocks). Marketing boards may also run or be in charge of quality-grading and assurance systems, as well as provide capacity building.
maximum residue level	The highest level of a pesticide residue that is legally tolerated in or on food or feed.
micro-economic	Relates to the single enterprise.
neoliberalism	Associated with policies of economic liberalization, privatization, deregulation, globalization, free trade and austerity.
organic	Here: A particular system of how to conduct agriculture, free from artificial industrial inputs and following defined principles of economic and social fairness as well as ecological diversity.
pandemic	Outbreak of infectious disease over a wide geographical area of high prevalence.
participatory guarantee system (PGS)	An alternative and complementary assurance system of certification based on a peer-review approach within social networks.
precautionary principle	Finding and fixing problems and hazards before they appear.

preferences in trade	Lowering tariffs when importing products, e.g. from low income countries, like the EU-GSP (Generalised System of Preferences).
premium	Some extra margin on top of the normal price for the benefit of producers.
Public-Private Partnership (PPP)	A cooperation by private initiatives with state support by financial or regulatory means.
restrictive business practices	Unfavourable terms of business imposed by buyers on the suppliers by virtue of market power.
smallholders	Small-scale family owned and run farm units, pastoralists and fishers, of 1 to 10 ha, relying on family labour and using part of their produce for home consumption.
spill-over-effect	Automatic transfer of knowledge or a certain practice from one area to another
supermarket	Bigger grocery of at least 400 m² sales floor, self-service and a cashpoint at the checkout.
supply chain	The flow of primary products through the different stages of processing and handling up to the point of final consumption.
supply management	Some kind of control over the sales' volume of a particular commodity, mostly to limit the supply on a market.
sustainability	To meet the needs of the present without compromising the ability of future generations to meet their own needs respecting planetary limits. For natural systems or resources sustainability denotes the reproductive capacity.
Sustainable Development Goals (SDG)	2015 adopted blueprint of the UN for the future worldwide course of socio-economic development with 17 major goals.
Technical Barriers to Trade (TBT)	Term of the WTO referring to trade discrimination due to unilaterally set requirements of products of qualitative nature.
third-party certification	The 'third-party' is supposed to be a neutral accredited outsider, not involved in the commercial exchange.
three Sisters	The three organizations, recognized by the WTO Agreement on Sanitary and Phyto-sanitary Measures (SPS) as international standard-setting organizations (Codex Alimentarius Commission, International Plant Protection Commission, and International Organization for Animal Health).
traceability	The ability to verify the history, location, or application of a product by means of documented identification.

transformational change	A radical change of the foundations and practices of a given system; here: in food and agriculture
treadmill effect	Referring to fierce economic constrains, which put strong pressure on producers to cope with competition.
voluntary partnership agreements (VPA)	An agreement among governments, which includes commitments and actions of both sides to halt trade in illegal goods (here in illegal timber).
Voluntary Sustainability Standard (VSS)	Here: Standards for the production of commodities, following private rules of sustainability, which producers comply with by own choice in order to access certain promising markets.
zoonotic disease (or zoonoses)	If harmful germs, generated from wild and/or domesticated animals, spread to people, where they cause a serious illness.

References

Ainsworth, C. and Carrington, D. (2000). BSE disaster: The history. *New Scientist*, 25 October. Available at: www.newscientist.com/article/dn91-bse-disaster-the-history/

Alliance for Corporate Transparency Project (2019). 2019 Research report: An analysis of the sustainability reports of 1000 companies pursuant to the EU Non-Financial Reporting Directive. Available at: http://www.allianceforcorporatetransparency.org/assets/2019_Research_Report%20_Alliance_for_Corporate_Transparency.pdf

Andersen, K.G., Rambaut, A., Lipkin, W.I., Holmes, E.C., and Garry, R.F. (2020). The proximal origin of SARS-CoV-2. *Nature Medicine*, 17 March. Available at: https://www.nature.com/articles/s41591-020-0820-9

Anderson, C., Pimbert, M., and Kiss, C. (2015). *Building, Defending and Strengthening Agroecology. A Global Struggle for Food Sovereignty.* ILEIA, Centre for Learning on Sustainable Agriculture, Wageningen.

Arvay, C.G. (2020). Wir können es besser: Wie Umweltzerstörung die Corona-Pandemie auslöste und warum ökologische Medizin unsere Rettung ist (German Edition) [*We Can Do Better: How Environmental Destruction Triggered the Corona Pandemic and Why Ecological Medicine Is Our Salvation*]. Quadriga Publishing, Berlin.

Berner, B. (2019). Bio-Boom – Welcher Preis-Aufschlag gerechtfertigt ist [Organic boom: What price premium is justified?]. *Plus Minus*, 6 March.

Bernstein, S. and Cashore, B. (2007). Can non-state global governance be legitimate? An analytical framework. *Regulation and Governance*, 1 (4), 347–371. Available at: https://onlinelibrary.wiley.com/doi/full/10.1111/j.1748-5991.2007.00021.x

Burrow, S. (2019). How can transnational corporations be held to account in a world of nation states? A binding UN treaty would be an important step. *Social Europe*, 28 October. Available at: www.socialeurope.eu/un-treaty-on-business-and-human-rights-vital-for-economic-and-social-justice

Brack, D. (2019). Towards sustainable cocoa supply chains: Regulatory options for the EU. Study for FERN, Tropendos International and Fairtrade, London. Available at: www.fern.org/news-resources/towards-sustainable-cocoa-supply-chains-regulatory-options-for-the-eu-1978/

Buntzel, R. (1992). Öko-Steuern als Ausweg aus der Agrarkrise? [*Are Eco-taxes a Way Out of the Agricultural Crisis?*]. Agrarsoziale Gesellschaft, Göttingen.

Buntzel, R. (2020). Die Wertschöpfungsketten im Ernährungsbereich sind kein Allerheilmittel [Value chains in the food sector are no panacea]. In: Specker, M. (ed.). *Almanach Entwicklungspolitik – Wege aus der Ernährungskirse [Almanac Development Policy – Ways out of the Food Crisis]*. Caritas Switzerland, Lucerne, pp. 129–141.

Buntzel, R. and Mari, F. (2016). *Gutes Essen – arme Erzeuger: Wie die Agrarwitschaft mit Standards die Nahrungsmärkte beherrscht [Good Food – Poor Producers: How Agro-business Reigns Food Markets with Standards]*. Oekom Publishers, Munich.

Buntzel-Cano, R. (2002). Die BSE-Krise und ihre internationale Dimension – Fragen und Antworten aus entwicklungspolitischer Sicht [*The BSE Crisis and Its International Dimension – Q&A from a Development Perspective*]. Misereor und EED, Aachen/Bonn.

Bush, L. (2013). *Review of Standards: Recipes for Reality*. The MIT Press, Cambridge, MA.

Changing Markets Foundation (2018). *The False Promise of Certification – How Certification is Hindering Sustainability in the Textiles, Palm Oil and Fisheries Industries*. London. Available at: http://changingmarkets.org/wp-content/uploads/2018/05/False-promise_full-report-ENG.pdf

Codex Alimentarius Commission (1999/2001). Guidelines for the Production, Processing, Labelling and Marketing of Organically Produced Foods, CAC/GL 32–199/Rev 1, 2001, Rome.

Committee on Sustainability Assessment (COSA) (2013). *The COSA Measuring Sustainability Report: Coffee and Cocoa in 12 Countries*. Philadelphia, PA. Available at: http://thecosa.org/wp-content/uploads/2014/01/The-COSA-Measuring-Sustainability-Report.pdf

Dale, G. (2011). Consumer behaviour. In: Mansvelt, J. and Robbins, P. (eds), *Encyclopedias: Green Consumerism: An A-to-Z Guide*. SAGE Publications, New York, pp. 73–79. Available at: https://sk.sagepub.com/reference/greenconsumerism

Datenblatt Fairer Handel (2019). [Data sheet fair trade]. Accessible at: www.forum-fairer-handel.de/fileadmin/user_upload/dateien/publikationen/materialien_des_ffh/ 2019_FFH_Datenblatt-Fairer-Handel.pdf

DeCicco, J.M., Liu, D.Y., Heo, J., et al. (2016). Carbon balance effects of U.S. biofuel production and use. *Climatic Change*, 138, 667–680. Available at: https://doi.org/10.1007/s10584-016-1764-4

Easterly, W. (2013). *The Tyranny of Experts*. Basic Books, New York.

Environmental Action Germany and Rainforest Foundation Norway (2020). Biofuels to the Fire: The impact of continued expansion of palm and soy oil demand through biofuel policy. Available at: https://d5i6is0eze552.cloudfront.net/documents/RF_report_biofuel_0320_eng_SP.pdf?mtime=20200310101137

EU (2010). Best Practice Guidelines for Voluntary Certification Schemes for Agricultural Products and Foodstuffs (2010/C 341/04). Available at: https://eur-lex.europa.eu/LexUriServ/ LexUriServ.do?uri=OJ:C:2010:341:0005:0011:en:PDF

EU (2019). Directive of the European Parliament and of the Council on Unfair Trading Practices in Business-to-Business Relationships in the Agricultural and Food Supply Chain (2019/ 633). Brussels, 17 April. Available at: https://eur-lex.europa.eu/legal-content/EN/TXT/ PDF/?uri=CELEX:32019L0633&from=en

European Commission (2020). *Progress Report on FLEGT Voluntary Partnership Agreements.* DG Environment, Brussels, 7 May. Available at: https://ec.europa.eu/environment/forests/ flegt.htm

European Court of Auditors (2016). The EU system for the certification of sustainable biofuels. Special Report, No. 18. Available at: https://www.eca.europa.eu/Lists/ECADocuments/ SR16_18/SR_BIOFUELS_EN.pdf

European Environmental Citizen's Organisation for Standardisation (ECOS) (2020). Standards in the time of the European Green Deal. Brussels, April. Available at: https:// ecostandard.org/wp-content/uploads/2020/04/ECOS-PAPER-Standards-in-the-time-of-the-European-Green-Deal.pdf

European Parliament (2021). European Parliament Resolution on a WTO-compatible EU carbon border adjustment mechanism, P9_TA(2021)0071, 10 March. Available at: https:// www.europarl.europa.eu/doceo/document/TA-9-2021-0071_EN.html

FAO (2004). *The State of Agricultural Commodity Markets.* Rome. Available at: http://www.fao.org/ 3/y5419e/y5419e00.pdf

FiBL/IFOAM (2019). *The World of Organic Agriculture – Statistics and Emerging Trends.* Frick, Switzerland. Available at: https://shop.fibl.org/CHen/2020-organic-world-2019.html

Fontan Sers, C. and Mughal, M. (2018). From Maputo to Malabo: Public Agricultural Spending and Food Security in Africa. HAL archives-ouvertes.fr. Available at: https://hal.archives-ouvertes.fr/hal-01844094/document

Foucault, M. (2004). Geschichte der Gouvernementalität 2. Die Geburt der Biopolitik [*The History of Governance 2 – The Childbirth of Bio-policy*]. Vorlesung am Collège de France 1978–1979, Suhrkamp Publishers, Frankfurt.

Fountain, A.C. and Huetz-Adams, F. (2018). *Cocoa Barometer 2018.* VOICE Network. Available at: www.voicenetwork.eu/wp-content/uploads/2019/08/Cocoabarometer2018_web4.pdf

Fountain, A.C. and Huetz-Adams, F. (2020a). Necessary Farm Gate Prices for a Living Income. Existing Living Income Reference Prices Are Too Low. Available at: www.voicenetwork.eu/ cocoa-barometer/

Fountain, A.C. and Huetz-Adams, F. (2020b) *Cocoa Barometer 2020.* VOICE Network. Available at: www.voicenetwork.eu/cocoa-barometer/

Freyer, B. and Bingen, J. (2014), Organic and non-organic farming: Is convergence possible? In: Constance, D.H., Renard, M. C. and Rivera-Ferre, M.G. (eds), *Alternative Agrifood Movements – Patterns of Convergence and Divergence, Research in Rural Sociology and Development*, Chapter 12. Emerald Group Publishing, pp. 281–310. Available at: https:// www.researchgate.net/publication/270881335_Organic_and_Non-Organic_Farming_Is_ Convergence_Possible

GATT (1979). Document L/4903: Decision on Differential and More Favourable Treatment, Reciprocity and Fuller Participation of Developing Countries, adopted on 28 November 1979.

Gibbon, P. (2003), *Commodities, Donors, Value-Chain Analysis and Upgrading*. Danish Institute for International Studies, Copenhagen.

Gibbon, P. (2004). The commodity question: New thinking on old problems, paper for FAO symposium. Cited in: Green, D. (2005). Conspiracy of silence: Old and new directions on commodities. Conference paper presented to the *Strategic Dialogue on Commodities, Trade, Poverty and Sustainable Development*, organized by ICTSD and IIED, Barcelona, pp. 28–29. Available at: https://pdfs.semanticscholar.org/3e39/2f90b23eb3657555979d3243765ea8af48fc.pdf

Giovannucci, D. (2014). Presentation of the first global review of the Committee on Sustainability Assessment (COSA). UNFSS event launching the *COSA Global Review and the 2014 Report of the State of Sustainability Initiatives*, Geneva, 31 January.

Glasbergen, P. (2018). Smallholders do not Eat Certificates. *Ecological Economics* 147, 243–252.

Göpel, M. (2020). *Unsere Welt neu denken: Eine Einladung* [*Rethinking Our World: An Invitation*]. Ullstein Publishers, Berlin

GRAIN (2020). Fresh markets are not to blame for the new corona virus outbreak, posted on 27 February. Available at: https://grain.org/e/6413

Green, D. (2005). Conspiracy of silence: Old and new directions on commodities. Conference paper presented to the *Strategic Dialogue on Commodities, Trade, Poverty and Sustainable Development*. Organized by ICTSD and IIED, Barcelona. Available at: https://pdfs.semanticscholar.org/3e39/2f90b23eb3657555979d3243765ea8af48fc.pdf

Gruère, G. (2013). A characterisation of environmental labelling and information schemes, *OECD Environment Working Papers*, No. 62. OECD Publishing, Paris. Available at: https://doi.org/10.1787/5k3z11hpdgq2-en

Haerlin, B., Fuchs, N., and Willing, O. (2018). Für einen integralen Produktivitätsbegriff und eine selbstbewusste Biobewegung. Ein Diskussionsbeitrag der Zukunftsstiftung Landwirtschaft in der GLS Treuhand zum Thema "Bio 3.0" [For an Integral Productivity Term and a Self-confident Organic Movement: A Discussion Paper of the Agricultural Future Foundation of the GLS Trust on the subject 'Organic 3.0']. Bochum, Germany. Available at: www.zukunftsstiftung-landwirtschaft.de/media/Dokumente_Aktuelle_Meldungen/ZSL_zu_bio_3_0_11Pkt.pdf

Heminthavong, K. (2015). *Canada's Supply Management System*. Library of Parliament Research Publications. Economics, Resources and International Affairs Division. Retrieved from: https://en.wikipedia.org/wiki/Supply_management_(Canada)

Hepburn, J. and Bellmann, C. (2014). The future of the green box measures. In: Meléndez-Ortiz, R., Bellmann, C., and Hepburn, J. (eds), *Tackling Agriculture in the Post Bali Context: A Collection of Short Essays*. ICTSD, Geneva. Available at: www.ictsd.org/sites/default/files/research/Tackling%20Agriculture%20in%20the%20Post-Bali%20 Context_0.pdf

Hoffmann, U. (2011). Assuring Food Security in Developing Countries under the Challenges of Climate Change: Key Trade and Development Issues of a Fundamental Transformation of Agriculture. *UNCTAD Discussion Paper*, No. 201 (UNCTAD/OSG/DP/2011/1). Available at: https://unctad.org/en/Docs/osgdp20111_en.pdf

Hoffmann, U. (2013). Agriculture at the crossroads: Assuring food security in developing countries under the challenges of global warming. In: *UNCTAD Trade and Environment Review 2013: Wake up Before it is Too Late – Make Agriculture Truly Sustainable Now for Food Security in a Changing Climate*. Geneva. Available at: https://unctad.org/en/PublicationsLibrary/ditcted2012d3_en.pdf

Hoffmann, U. and Grothaus, F. (2015). Assuring Coherence between the Market-access and Livelihood Impact of Private Sustainability Standards. *UNFSS Discussion Paper*, No. 6. Geneva. Available at: https://unfss.org/wp-content/uploads/2013/02/unfss-discussion-paper-6-final-28may-2015.pdf

Hoffmann, U. and Vossenaar, R. (2007). Challenges and Opportunities arising from Private Standards on Food Safety and Environment for Exporters of Fresh Fruit and Vegetables in Asia: Experiences of Malaysia, Thailand and Viet Nam. Study for UNCTAD (document UNCTAD/DITC/TED/2007/6). Geneva. Available at: https://unctad.org/en/Docs/ditcted20076_en.pdf. On Kenya: www.globalgap.org/uk_en/media-events/news/articles/GLOBALG.A.P.-Farm-Assurer-Trains-Kenyan-Ministry-of-Agriculture-Officers/

IPE (2018). Green Supply Chain Map. Available at: http://wwwen.ipe.org.cn/MapBrand/Brand.aspx?q=6

IPES-Food (2017). International Panel of Experts on Sustainable Food Systems. *Too Big to Feed: Exploring the Impacts of Mega-mergers, Concentration, Concentration of Power in the Agri-food Sector*. Brussels. Available at: http://www.ipes-food.org/_img/upload/files/Concentration_ExecSummary.pdf

ISO and IEC (2004). ISO/IEC Guide 2 Standardization and Related Activities – General Vocabulary. ISO and IEC, Geneva.

ISEAL Alliance (2011). *The ISEAL 100 Survey Results – Business and Certification: Beyond the Tipping Point*. London. See: http://www.ecolabelindex.com/news/2011/03/07/the-iseal-100-survey-results/

ITC (2016). *Social and Environmental Standards: Contributing to More Sustainable Value Chains*. Geneva. Available at: http://www.intracen.org/uploadedFiles/intracenorg/ Content/ Publications/1ITC-EUI_Social_environmental_ standards_Low-res.pdf

ITC, IISD, FiBL (2019). *The State of Sustainability Markets 2019: Statistics and Emerging Trends*. Geneva. Available at: www.intracen.org/uploadedFiles/intracenorg/Content/Publications/Sustainabile markets 2019 web.pdf

ITC, IISD, FiBL (2020). *The State of Sustainability Markets 2020: Statistics and Emerging Trends*. Geneva. Available at: www.intracen.org/uploadedFiles/intracenorg/Content/Publications/SustainableMarkets2020-layout_20201012_web.pdf

ITC/EUI (2016). *Social and Environmental Standards: Contributing to More Sustainable Value Chains*. Geneva. pp. 17–18. Available at: http://www.intracen.org/uploadedFiles/intracenorg/Content/Publications/1ITC-EUI_Social_environmental_standards_Low-res.pdf

Joint Conference Church and Development (2015). Plädoyer für gerechte und nachhaltige globale Lebensmittelstandards [*A Plea for Just and Sustainable Global Food Standards*]. Schriftenreihe Heft 61, Bonn/Berlin.

Kox, H.L.M. (1993). *International Commodity-Related Environmental Agreements and the GATT System of Trade Rules*. Research Memorandum 1993–76. Free University, Amsterdam.

Krauss, J. and Krishnan, A. (2016). Global Decisions and Local Realities: Priorities and Producers' Upgrading Opportunities in Agricultural Global Production Networks. *UNFSS Discussion Paper* No. 7. Available at: https://unfss.files.wordpress.com/2013/02/discussion-paper_unfss_krausskrishnan_dec2016.pdf

Living Income (2020). Living Income Community of Practice. Available at: www.living-income.com/

LMC International (2020). *Cocoa: The Global Market Outlook for Beans, Butter, Liquor & Powder, 2020 Brochure.* Available at: www.lmc.co.uk/reports/cocoa-the-global-market/

Long, S. (2017). Competition Law and Sustainability: A Study of Industry Attitudes towards Multi-stakeholder Collaboration in the UK Grocery sector. Fairtrade Foundation, London.

Lunenborg, P. (2009). EPA General Exceptions undermine WTO negotiations on commodities. ICTSD, *Trade Negotiations Insights*, 8 (2). Available at: https://ictsd.iisd.org/bridges-news/trade-negotiations-insights/news/epa-general-exceptions-undermine-wto-negotiations-on

Malm, A. (2020). *Corona, Climate, Chronic Emergency: War Communism in the Twenty-First Century.* Verso Books.

Marx, A. (2017). The public-private distinction in global governance: How relevant is it in the case of voluntary sustainability standards? *The Chinese Journal of Global Governance*, 3 (1), 3, 12.

Marx, A., Lein, B., Sharma, A., Suse, A.G., Willemyns, I., Ebert, F., and Wouters, J. (2018). What Role Can Voluntary Sustainability Standards play in the European Union's GSP Scheme? Leuven Centre for Global Governance Studies. Available at: https://ghum.kuleuven.be/ggs/publications/research_reports/report-vvs-and-gsp.pdf

Mattli, W. and Büthe, T. (2003). Setting international standards: Technological rationality or primacy of power? *World Politics*, 56 (1), 3–4.

Mavroidis, P. C. and Robert, W. (2016). *Private standards and the WTO: Reclusive no more.* EUI Working Paper RSCAS 2016/17, Florence: European University Institute.

Migliorini, P. and Wezel, A. (2017). Converging and Diverging Principles and Practices of Agricultural Regulations and Agroecology, *Agronomic Sustainable Development*, 37, 63.

Molenaar, J.W., Beekmans, A., and Pelders, P. (2011). Producer groups models and certification: An exploration of various producer group models in the agricultural and forestry sectors. Available at: www.aidenvironment.org/media/uploads/documents/A2192_ISEAL_Producer_Group_Models_and_ Certification.pdf

Murphy-Bokern, D. and Kleemann, L. (2015). The role of corporate social responsibility in reducing greenhouse gas emissions from agriculture and food. Study for the International Food Policy Research Institute, p. 21. Available at: http://www.murphy-bokern.com/images/IFPRI_CR_Report_July_2015.pdf

Neghi, A. (2020). The World Trade Organization and sustainability standards. In: Neghi, A., Pérez-Pineda, J.A., and Blankenbach, J. (eds), *Sustainability Standards and Global Governance – Experiences of Emerging Economies.* Springer, Singapore, p. 49. Available at: https://link.springer.com/book/10.1007/978-981-15-3473-7

Neghi, A., Pérez-Pineda, J.A., and Blankenbach, J. (eds) (2020). *Sustainability Standards and Global Governance – Experiences of Emerging Economies.* Springer, Singapore.

Nelson, V. and Martin, A. (2013). Assessing the poverty impact of sustainability standards. Natural Resources Institute, University of Greenwich, London, p. 104. Available at: www.nri.org/images/documents/development-programmes/sustainable_trade/Assessing ThePovertyImpactOfSustainabilityStandards.pdf

Niggli, U., Plagge, J., Reese, S., et al. (2015). Towards Modern Sustainable Agriculture with Organic Farming as the Leading Model. A Discussion Document on Organic 3.0, Second Draft, 30 September.

OECD (2002). Regulatory Policies in OECD Countries: From Interventionism to Regulatory Governance. *OECD Reviews of Regulatory Reform*. OECD Publishing, Paris. Available at: https://doi.org/10.1787/9789264177437-en

Opeyemi Ayinde (2014). Is Marketing Board a Barrier or a Stimulant of Agricultural Production in West Africa? A Comparative Study of Ghana and Nigeria Cocoa Pricing Eras. *Ghana Journal of Development Studies*, 11 (2). Available at: https://www.ajol.info/index.php/gjds/article/view/112245/102002

Overdevest, C. and Zeitlin, J. (2016). Experimentalism in Transnational Forest Law Enforcement Governance and Trade (FLEGT) Voluntary Partnership Agreements in Indonesia and Ghana. Amsterdam Centre for Contemporary European Studies, *SSRN Research Paper* 2016/02.

Oxfam (2018). *Ripe for Change: Ending Human Suffering in Supermarket Supply Chains*. Cowley, Oxford. Available at: https://policy-practice.oxfam.org.uk/publications/ripe-for-change-ending-human-suffering-in-supermarket-supply-chains-620418

Partzsch, L., Zander, M., and Robinson, H. (2019). Cotton certification in Sub-Saharan Africa: Promotion of environmental sustainability or greenwashing? *Global Environmental Change*, 57, 101924, 8. Available at: https://reader.elsevier.com/reader/sd/pii/ S095937801830785 4?token=A05AC1C3E306D11368339C6207B23BD0D329F722F6 DEA19679A546800 0330A1543255319BBFC95797F5D3C453DB044B9

Politico Morning Trade Europe (2020). Issue of 28 October. Available at: www.politico.eu

Ponte, S. and Gibbon, P. (2005). Quality standards, conventions and the governance of global value chains. *Economy and Society*, 34 (1), 1–31.

Potts, J., Lynch, M., Wilkings, A., Huppé, G., Cunningham, M., and Voora, V. (2014). *The State of Sustainability Initiatives 2014, Standards and the Green Economy*. Available at: http://www.iisd.org/sites/default/files/pdf/2014/ssi_2014.pdf

Power, M. (1999). *The Audit Society: Rituals of Verification*. Oxford University Press, Oxford. For a review see: www.developmenteducationreview.com/issue11-review2

Quammens, D. (2013). *Spillover: Animal Infections and the Next Human Pandemic*. New York Times Publishing. New York. Available at: https://skenevik.centercityoperatheater.org/file-ready/spillover-animal-infections-and-the-next-human-pandemic

Reuters (2019). Ivory Coast, Ghana lift threat to cocoa sustainability schemes, 23 October. Available at: www.reuters.com/article/us-ivory-coast-ghana-cocoa/ivory-coast-ghana-lift-threat-to-cocoa-sustainability-schemes-idUSKBN1X224R

Rousset, S., Deconinck, K., Jeong, H., and Von Lampe, M. (2015). Voluntary environmental and organic standards in agriculture: Policy implications. *OECD Food, Agriculture and Fisheries Papers* No. 86. Available at: www.oecd-ilibrary.org/docserver/5jrw8fg0rr8x-en.pdf?expires =1589377875&id=id&accname=guest&checksum=A8794BD022135FADDFCF1B0B2BE 0C9E4

Rundgren, G. (2011a). Eco labels: The more successful, the less value. 30 December. *Garden Earth Blogspot.* Available at: https://gardenearth.blogspot.com/2011/12/eco-labels-more-successful-less-value.html

Rundgren, G. (2011b). What gives value to an eco label? *Garden Earth Blogspot.* Available at: https://gardenearth.blogspot.com/2011/03/what-gives-value-to-eco-label.html

Rundgren, G. (2015). *Global Eating Disorder.* Regeneration, Uppsala.

Rundgren, G. (2017). Can we shop our way to a better world? *Garden Earth Blogspot,* 9 August. Available at: https://gardenearth.blogspot.com/2013/04/can-we-shop-our-way-to-better-world.html

Rundgren, G. (2020). Ask a reductionist question and you will get a reductionist answer. *Garden Earth Blogspot,* 20 March. Available at: https://gardenearth.blogspot.com/2020/03/ask-reductionist-question-and-you-will.html

Sadhu, S., Kysia, K., Onyango, L., Zinnes, C., Lord, S., Monnard, A., and Arellano, I.R. (2020). Assessing Progress in Reducing Child Labor in Cocoa Production in Cocoa Growing Areas of Côte d'Ivoire and Ghana. NORC at the University of Chicago, Chicago, IL. Available at: www.norc.org/PDFs/Cocoa Report/NORC 2020 Cocoa Report_English.pdf

Salter, R., Gonzalez, C.G., and Kronk Warner, E.A. (eds) (2018). *An Environmental Justice Critique of Biofuels. Energy Justice: US and International Perspectives.* Edward Elgar Publishing, Cheltenham.

Sarasin, P. (2020). Mit Foucault die Pandemie verstehen [Understanding the pandemic with Foucault], 25 March. Available at: https://geschichtedergegenwart.ch/mit-foucault-die-pandemie-verstehen/

Schader, C., Grenz, J., Meier, M.S., and Stolze, M. (2014). Scope and precision of sustainability assessment approaches to food systems. *Ecology and Society* 19(3): 42. Available at: www.ecologyandsociety.org/vol19/iss3/art42/

Segarra, A.E. and Rawson, J.M. (2001). *Mad Cow Disease: Agricultural Issues.* Congressional Research Service, Report for the Congress, 12 March.

Sennholz-Weinhardt, B. (2019). Schwarzer Tee, Weisse Weste: Menschenrechtsverletzungen auf Teeplantagen in Assam und die Verantwortung deutscher Unternehmen [*Clean Slate: Human Rights' Violations in Tea Estates in Assam and the Responsibility of German Companies*]. Oxfam (Germany). Available at: www.oxfam.de/assam-tee

Siegner, C. (2019). Foodborne illnesses are on the rise, US Center for Disease Control and Prevention finds. *Food Drive,* Washington, DC, 29 April. Available at: www.fooddive.com/news/foodborne-illnesses-are-on-the-rise-cdc-finds/553585/

Slavin, T. (2018). Deadline 2020: 'We won't end deforestation through certification schemes', brands admit. Reuters Events: Sustainable Business (posted on 1 November). Available at: www.ethicalcorp.com/deadline-2020-we-wont-end-deforestation-through-certification-schemes-brands-admit

Sligh, M. and Cierpka, T. (2007). Organic Values. In: Lockeretz, W. (ed.), *Organic Farming – An International History.* Cambridge University Press. Chapter 3, pp. 30–40.

Squatrito, S., Arena, E., Palmeri, R., and Biagio, F. (2020). Public and private standards in crop production: Their role in ensuring safety and sustainability, *Sustainability 2020,* 12, 606. Available at: https://www.mdpi.com/2071-1050/12/2/606/pdf

Subramanian, S. (2019). Is fair trade finished? *The Guardian*, 23 July. Available at: www.theguardian.com/business/2019/jul/23/fairtrade-ethical-certification-supermarkets-sainsburys

Tate, W.B. (1994). The development of the organic industry and market: An International perspective. In: Lampkin, N.H. and Padel, S. (eds), *The Economics of Organic Farming – An International Perspective*. CABI. Part 1, section 2.

Tayleur, C., Balmford, A., Buchanan, G.M., et al. (2018). Where are commodity crops certified, and what does it mean for conservation and poverty alleviation? *Biological Conservation*, 217, pp. 36–46. Available at: https://www.sciencedirect.com/science/article/pii/S0006 320716309582

Tittonell, P. (2014). Ecological intensification of agriculture – Sustainable by nature. *Current Opinion in Environmental Sustainability*, 8, 53. Available at: www.sciencedirect.com

TransSustain (2019). *Policy Brief, Voluntary Coffee Standards Index: The Independent Guide to Sustainability Certifications in the Coffee Sector*. Available at:www.uni-muenster.de/imperia/md/content/transsustain/vocsi_policy_brief_wwu.pdf

TransSustain (2020). Combining sustainability certifications to improve livelihoods: Lessons from Colombian coffee cooperatives. TransSustain Policy Brief, posted on 20 January. Available at: www.uni-muenster.de/imperia/md/content/ transsustain/trans_sustain_-_colombia_policy_brief.pdf

Trinkwalder, S. (2016). *Fairarscht: Wie Wirtschaft und Handel die Kunden für dumm verkaufen [Fair-misled: How Business and Commerce Fool Their Customers]*. Knaur Publishers, Munich.

Tropenbos, EcoCare Ghana, Forest Watch Ghana and Fern (2018). Transferring Lessons from FLEGT-VPA to Promote Governance Reform in Ghana's Cocoa Sector. Tropendos International and Fairtrade. London. Available at: www.fern.org/news-resources/towards-sustainable-cocoa-supply-chains-regulatory-options-for-the-eu-1978/

Umair Muhammad (2016). *Confronting Injustice: Social Activism in the Age of Individualism*. Haymarket Books. Chicago, IL. Accessible at: www.climateandcapitalism.com/2016/04/20/ethical-consumerism-or-social-activism

UNCTAD (1995). Sustainable development and the possibilities for the reflection of environmental costs in prices. Report by the UNCTAD secretariat to the Standing Committee on Commodities. Document TD/B/CN.1/29. Available at: https://works.bepress.com/henk_kox/31/

UNCTAD (2003). *Economic Development in Africa: Trade Performance and Commodity Dependence*. UNCTAD, Geneva.

UNCTAD (2013). *Trade and Environment Review 2013, Wake-up before it is Too Late: Make Agriculture Truly Sustainable Now for Food Security in a Changing Climate*. UNCTAD, Geneva. Available at: http://unctad.org/en/pages/PublicationWebflyer.aspx?publicationid=666

UNCTAD (2015). The role of competition policy in promoting sustainable and inclusive growth. Document TD/RBP/CONF.8/6. Available at: https://unctad.org/meetings/en/SessionalDocuments/tdrbpconf8d6_en.pdf

UNEP (2016). *UNEP Frontiers 2016 Report, Emerging Issues of Environmental Concern*. UNEP, Nairobi.

Vogl, C.R., Kilcher, L., and Schmidt, H.P. (2005). Are standards and regulations of organic farming moving away from small farmers' knowledge? *Journal of Sustainable Agriculture*, 26, 1–26. Available at: www.researchgate.net/publication/241746720_Are_Standards_and_ Regulations_of_Organic_Farming_Moving_Away_from_Small_Farmers'_Knowledge

VOICE Network (2019a). Certification is not the systemic solution to unsustainable cocoa. Position Paper. Available at: www.voicenetwork.eu/cocoa-barometer/

VOICE Network (2019b). Voice Network welcomes historic move to raise cocoa prices, questions remain on implementation. Position Paper. Available at: www.voicenetwork.eu/ cocoa-barometer/

Vorley, B. (2013). Markets for many rather than the few. *Rural21*, No. 2/2013, p. 29. Available at: www.rural21.com/fileadmin/downloads/2013/en-02/rural2013_02-S28-29.pdf

Vorley, B. and Proctor, F. (2008). Inclusive Business in Agrifood Markets: Evidence and Action. IIED project on Regoverning Markets: Small-scale Producers in Modern Agrifood Markets – Evidence and Action. Available at: https://pubs.iied.org/pdfs/16503IIED.pdf

Waarts, Y. (2014). Benefits for smallholder tea producers in Kenya. Impact assessment of farmer field schools including training for rainforest alliance certification. The Agricultural Economics Research Institute. Paper presented at the Workshop on Effectiveness of Voluntary Sustainability Standards, Leuven Centre for Global Governance Studies, 1–3 October. Report of the Workshop. Accessible at: www.esf.org/coordinating-research/ exploratory-workshops/social-sciences-soc/workshops-detail.html?ew=13273

Weissinger, R. (2021). Standards and the international standardization landscape: Relevance to plastics. Research Paper, Graduate Institute of International and Development Studies, Geneva. July.

Wezel, A., Brives, H., Casagrande, M., Clément, C., Dufour, A., and Vandenbroucke, P. (2016). Agroecology territories: Places for sustainable agricultural and food systems and biodiversity conservation. *Agroecology and Sustainable Food Systems*, 40 (2), 132–144. Available at: https:// doi.org/10.1080/21683565.2015.1115799

WTO (1994). Agreement on Technical Barriers to Trade, Annex 1: Terms and their Definitions for the Purpose of this Agreement. Available at: www.wto.org/english/docs_e/legal_e/17-tbt_e.htm

ZDFInfo Doku (2020). Schokolade – Das bittere Geschäft [Chocolate – The Bitter Business]. ZDF documentary. Available at: www.zdf.de/dokumentation/zdfinfo-doku/-schokolade-das-bittere-geschaeft-100.html

Index

A

Accreditation 12, 13, 36
Agenda 19, 20
Agreement on Sanitary and Phyto-
    Sanitary Measures (SPS
    Agreement) 11, 29, 38, 39
Agreement on Technical Barriers to
    Trade (TBT Agreement) 6, 10, 20,
    38, 39, 40
Agro-ecological production 18, 35, 42
Agro-forestry 18, 42, 52

B

Biofuels 35, 105, 106
BSE epidemic / crisis 24, 110, 111, 116
Business to business (B2B) standards 13,
    22, 23, 25, 38, 49, 71, 117
Business to consumer (B2C)
    standards 13, 117

C

Certification 11, 12, 13, 16, 17, 19, 26,
    30, 31, 33, 34, 36, 37, 39, 43, 44,
    45, 50, 51, 55, 56, 57, 58, 59, 60, 61,
    89, 93, 94, 99, 101, 102, 103, 106,
    108, 109, 114
Child labour XII 26, 27, 33, 67, 84,
    88, 106
Codex Alimentarius
    Commission 7, 40, 55
Co-governance systems 20
Commodification 2
Community-supported agriculture 28,
    54, 101
Competition policy 80, 84, 85, 104, 120
Concept of 'like products' 10
Conformity assessment XII 12, 13, 14,
    15, 16, 31, 38, 98, 128
Consumers' willingness to pay 50
Contract farming 44, 45, 128
Control point(s) 15, 23, 25, 35, 40

Co-regulation 99, 106
Corona crisis 110, 116
Cost-treadmill effect/ trap 25, 27, 51, 72, 101, 118
Counter-consumerism 21
Credence values 9, 13, 20

D

Dedicated producer(s)/ supplier(s) 23, 44, 64
Due diligence requirements/ regulation 24, 65, 78, 80, 86, 87, 88, 89, 102, 108, 110, 113, 120, 128

E

Eco-label(s) 9, 21, 36, 93, 94
Epidemic(s) 24, 109, 110, 111, 113, 114, 115, 117, 128
EU Directive 7, 85, 86
EU Forest Law Enforcement Governance and Trade Program (FLEGT) 106, 107, 108, 109
EU Generalised Scheme of (trade) Preferences 95
EU Regulation 7, 54, 95, 100
EU Renewable Energy Directive (RED) 105
European Committee for Standardization (CEN) 8
European Green New Deal 99

F

Farmer livelihoods 32, 33, 45, 47, 73, 108
Food and Agricultural Organization of the UN (FAO) 3, 4, 7, 81, 123

Food miles/ mileage 54, 128
Food scares 24, 25
Formal and non-formal system of standard creation 8, 9, 13, 14
Fundamental transformation of agriculture 28, 35

G

GlobalGAP standard 12, 14, 23, 41, 46, 48, 53, 59
Green and ethical consumerism 1, 2, 6, 20, 21, 22, 29, 53
Green growth 2
Green economy 2, 26, 118, 129
Greenwashing XII 2, 64, 103, 129
Growth paradigm 20, 37, 118

H

Hazard Analysis and Critical Control Points (HACCP) 24, 25, 124
Horizontal problem shifting 35
Hyper globalization 115

I

IFOAM Basic Standards 41
Informal food market(s) 47, 115
Internal control system 61
Internalization of environmental and social externalities / cost internalization XII 27, 45, 51, 94, 99
International Commodity Agreement(s) 90, 91, 124
International Commodity-related Environment Agreement(s) 91, 124

International Federation of Organic
Agriculture Movements (IFOAM –
Organics International) 41, 52, 124
International Plant Protection
Convention 7, 40, 130
International Social and Environmental
Accreditation and Labelling Alliance
(ISEAL Alliance) 9, 36, 37, 124
International standard 10, 15, 39, 40,
41, 55, 117
International standard setting
organisations/ bodies 7, 11, 40,
55, 130
International Standardization
Organization (ISO) 5, 6, 7, 8, 9, 13,
14, 25, 31, 124
International supply/ value chain(s)
XI 20, 22, 23, 43, 48, 80, 90, 102

L

Label fatigue 2, 64
Label overload 2
Land registration 44
Legitimate objective 39
Lifestyle-centric activism 22
Limits to growth 19, 20, 101
Living income and wage XII 35, 37,
52, 65, 66, 67, 90, 92, 93, 118,
120, 129

M

Marginalization of smallholder
farmers 42, 50, 90, 118, 119
Market concentration 50, 69, 70, 79,
101, 120
Market surveillance 12, 13
Marketing boards 28, 80, 81, 82, 83,
90, 129

Maximum residue level(s)
(MRL) 48, 124
Metrology 12
Modern indulgence trade 2

N

National commodity board(s) 47, 81
National interpretative guidelines 41
National standard organizations 14
Neo-liberalism 20, 93, 129
Non-product-related processes and
production methods 3, 10, 20, 21

O

Organized, formal food market(s) 47

P

Pandemic(s) 109, 110, 111, 112, 113,
115, 116, 129
Participatory guarantee system(s)
(PGS) 61, 129
Plant-protection management 41, 73
Power asymmetry XII 27
Price premium(s) 4, 27, 49, 58, 67, 68,
71, 72, 92, 94, 104, 118
Principles of non-discriminatory
treatment 10
Private standards 3, 8, 9, 10, 11, 29, 100
Producer groups (of farmers) 28,
43, 44, 89
Productivity 26, 27, 31, 35, 43, 45, 50,
51, 60, 73, 74, 75, 79, 83, 84, 90, 91,
115, 118, 119
Product characteristics 9, 10, 13, 20, 37
Proliferation (of VSS) 11, 30, 72
Public goods and services 28, 101

Public-private partnerships 20, 101, 130

Public procurement 49, 119

Public stockholding programmes 81

Q

Quality infrastructure 12, 14

Quality premium(s) 2, 43, 45

R

Recognized needs test 38

Remunerative prices 2, 58, 129

Resilience of agriculture 33

Resource mining 26, 51, 74

Restrictive business and trade practices 58, 72, 85, 86, 120

Rio Declaration 19, 20

Rural poverty 18, 44, 118

S

Scientific justifiability of standard claims 38

Seed regulation(s) 44

Self-control / self-declaration 13, 109

Smallholder farmers/ smallholders 23, 29, 32, 35, 37, 44, 45, 47, 48, 50, 51, 59, 61, 72, 77, 81, 83, 118, 128, 130

Speculation with farmland 35, 59

Standardizing body 10

Sufficiency 37, 38, 118

Supply chain governance 22

Sustainability certificates 9

Sustainable Development Goals (SDGs) 29, 130

T

Technical specification 7, 14

Testing protocols 14, 40

Third-party conformity assessment/ certification system 36, 63, 64, 102, 130

Traditional (farming) knowledge 54, 59, 60, 101

Transformational change 2, 3, 22, 26, 29, 32, 33, 77, 79, 89, 99, 113, 120, 131

U

UN Conference on Environment and Development (UNCED) 19

UN Forum on Sustainability Standards (UNFSS) 3, 34

V

VSS impact assessment 31, 36

W

World Organization for Animal Health 7, 40

World Trade Organization (WTO) 3, 5, 6, 7, 10, 11, 20, 27, 29, 38, 39, 40, 42, 46, 49, 55, 81, 84, 85, 93, 105, 120, 130

Z

Zoonotic disease(s) / zoonosis 112, 113, 114, 115, 131

Lightning Source UK Ltd.
Milton Keynes UK
UKHW021434081121
393611UK00004B/9